Thai Insi

An Insider's Guide to the Best of Thailand

By Granville Kirkup and Robert Wisehart

Copyright

Contents

Chiang Mai City Map 4

1   Welcome to Chiang Mai 7
2   Your First Visit to Thailand? 13
3   Thai Culture and Customs 17
4   Hotels 23
5   Getting About 33
6   Things to do 47
7   Restaurants 57
8   Bars and Clubs 75
9   Shopping 83
10 Sports & Fitness 91
11 Massage & Personal Care 101
12 Thai Food 107
13 Two or Three Days in Chiang Mai 111
14 Staying Longer 119
15 Out of Town Trips 123
16 Some Thai Phrases 131
17 Useful Chiang Mai Information 137
18 Authors Bios 145
19 Acknowledgments 147
20 Further Reading 149

Chiang Mai City Maps

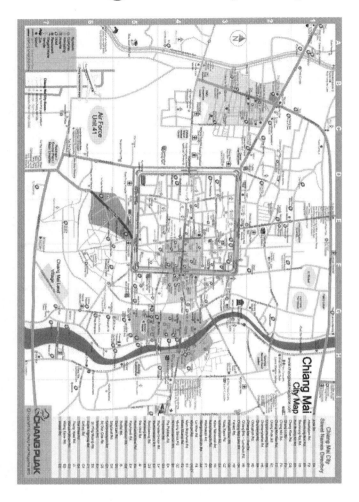

Maps

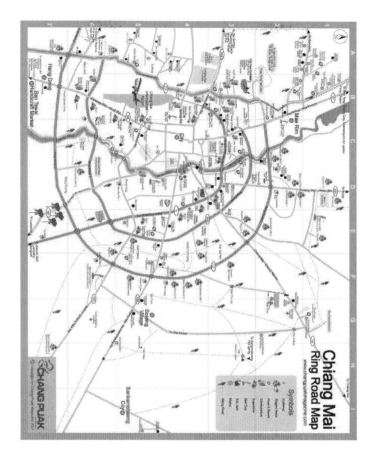

Thai Insider: Chiang Mai

1: Welcome to Chiang Mai

Chiang Mai is Thailand's second largest city and its northern capital. Just 55 minutes by plane from Bangkok, it is also Thailand's second most-popular tourist attraction. But while Bangkok teems with a population of 8.5 million, (some unofficial estimates much higher), Chiang Mai's population of only 1.5 million makes the two cities very different

With its smaller size and population, Chiang Mai is an easy city to get around in. Tuk-tuks and songthaews (small motorized vehicles used as taxis) are easy to find and cheap and most popular tourist destinations are close to the inner walled city. There are over 300 temples to explore in the area. The Ping River runs through the city, and there are many good riverfront restaurants. There are sights to see and elephants to ride.

Most of the people speak Kham Muang or northern Thai. About 85 percent of the population is Buddhist. To avoid offense, tourists should dress respectfully, especially when visiting temples – remove your shoes and cover your shoulders when visiting a temple.

In this book you will learn about the best hotels and restaurants, from budget-friendly to five-star. We will tell you the best places to go and how to get there – both in town and for day trips to the surrounding area. We'll tell you the best places to shop, in malls or markets, and how not to get ripped off! We will tell you about the best bars and restaurants and where to listen to live music at night. As a bonus, there are hundreds of 'Insider tips' written by locals and frequent Chiang Mai visitors.

Insider tip: The best Chiang Mai map is Nancy Chandler's 'Map of Chiang Mai', available at bookstores, hotel gift shops, and from Amazon.com. (About $15.95) It shows almost all hotels and restaurants plus the sightseeing attractions in town and in the surrounding area. *Nancychandler.net*

Insider tip: City Life Magazine is published monthly and available at news stands and many restaurants. Photographer Steve Yarnold attends most social events in town and publishes a weekly newsletter called 'Coming Up', with all the social and restaurant events in the coming weeks. You can get a copy by emailing Steve at *charityrooftopparty@gmail.com*. Another local magazine is *Chang Puak*, available free and published in English and French, with a useful current guide to restaurants and bars.

All the Chiang Mai history you really need to know

In the late 13th century the Lanna Kingdom (then a separate country) covered most of what is now northern Thailand. Chiang Mai was built in 1296 by King Mengrai as the capital of the Lanna Kingdom. The name means

'New City'. The city was overthrown by Burma in 1557, and returned to the Lanna Kingdom in the war of 1774, when Siam's King Taksin sent the Burmese home for good. The Lanna Kingdom itself became a part of Siam in 1892, and in 1949 Siam became known as Thailand. Until the early part of the 20th century, Chiang Mai could only be visited by river or by elephant.

The Ping River

The Ping River originates in the Chiang Dao mountains on the Thai / Myanmar (Burma) border, then flows down through villages and Chiang Mai to join the Chao Phraya River which runs through Bangkok. There is no commercial traffic on the Ping River in Chiang Mai, just a few small tourist river cruise boats.

The best time to visit

Chiang Mai has a 'tropical wet and dry' climate. November through February are the best months to visit – the cooler months, and when the flowers are blooming. Temperatures range from 70F to 80F (21C to 26C) and there is little rain this time of year. The summer months are hotter (over 100F, or 37C) and bring more rain. Chiang Mai is cooler than Bangkok.

Insider tip: March can be smoky and polluted because of the burning of rice fields in the area. Songkran in mid-April is a festival that involves water fights and pelting locals and tourists with water and flour. If you are out and about you will get wet!

Today's Chiang Mai includes shopping malls, trendy boutiques, high-rise apartments and riverside restaurants offering both Thai and western cuisine.

Enjoy your trip to Chiang Mai – for many, their favorite part of Thailand, to which they always want to return!

2: Your First Visit to Thailand?

Passport and visas

To enter Thailand you need a passport with the expiration date of at least six months after the end of your Thailand trip. A visa is not necessary if your stay is no longer than 30 days (29 nights). For longer stays you need to get a visa from a Thai embassy or consulate. Details can be found online at *Thaiembassy.com*.

A new METV visa was introduced in 2015. (Multiple Entry Tourist Visa). Visitors of any nationality can apply for a multiple-entry tourist visa valid for six months, with a stay per entry of up to 60 days. The cost of this visa is 5,000 baht. ($145 or £92)

Thailand is usually entered via Bangkok, but there are also direct flights to Chiang Mai, Phuket and Koh Samui. Some of these flights depart from Hong Kong and Seoul Korea.

Events and festivals

January: Bo Sang Village Umbrella Festival.

February: Chiang Mai Flower Festival, a three-day festival held every year during the first weekend in February.

April: Songkran New Year water celebrations and water fights. If you are out, you will get drenched by supersoakers!

November: Loi Krathong. Can be translated as 'To float a basket', which comes from the tradition of floating decorated floating baskets traditionally made from banana leaves called 'Krathong' in rivers and ponds. In Chiang Mai the festival is also celebrated by launching thousands of 'khom loi' fire balloons into the sky. The party lasts for three days.

Insider tip: Khom loi (fire balloons) used to be sent into the sky in their thousands on all three days, but a new law in 2015 restricted this to 9pm – midnight on the main day of Loi Krathong only, as Khom Loi can be a danger to aircraft.

December: King's birthday. The King is much revered.

Religion

Buddhism (95%). Other religions include Muslim (3.8%) Hinduism (0.1%) and Christianity (0.5%).

Language

The language spoken is Thai, with some regional differences, including some Northern Thai (Kham Muang) in the Chiang Mai area. English is widely spoken in hotels and restaurants.

Food and drink

Thai food can be very spicy, but Chiang Mai's food is usually less spicy than that of the northeast or the south. Many restaurants also serve western food.

Don't drink Thai tap water, even to clean your teeth. Use bottled water. Water and iced served in restaurants are usually OK – certainly in the main tourist spots.

Shopping

Shopping options range from market stalls to air-conditioned malls. There are many bargains to be had, and haggling is expected in markets and smaller stores. (Not in shopping malls.)

Insider tip: When haggling, be relaxed and cheerful. Smile or laugh at the first price offered, and offer about half. Expect to end up around two thirds of the first offered price. Don't haggle down to the last 10 baht – that is only 30 cents. The vendors need to make a living!

Collectors can find antiques from Thailand, Burma, Cambodia and Laos. Be warned, there are many fakes. It's forbidden to take any Buddha image out of Thailand without a permit.

Thai Baht

The exchange rate for Thai baht fluctuates, but for this book a rate of approximately 35 baht to the US dollar is used, or 54 baht to the British pound.

You can exchange your local currency for Thai baht at many 'change money' places in town (for example, there are several near the Night Bazaar). There are also many ATMs, which will dispense Thai baht.

[16]

3: Thai Culture and Customs

Thailand is a fun and easy-going country, but a basic understanding of the country's culture and customs makes travel more interesting and helps to avoid giving offense.

Head, feet and shoes

The head is the most sacred part of the body in Thailand, so do not touch people on the head, even children.

The feet are the 'unclean' part of the body, so avoid pointing your feet at people, especially monks if you are sitting in a temple. Tuck them underneath you or fold your legs to one side.

Remove your shoes before going into a house or temple building. Hotel staff will always remove their shoes before coming into your room. Do the same if you are 'just looking' at a hotel room. For this reason, slip-on shoes for men are best in Thailand.

The King

The king is much revered in Thailand (they usually refer to him as 'my King'), so always be respectful to the king and the royal family. Almost every home and business has a photograph of the king on the wall. There are strict *Lese Majeste* laws making it a serious offence to speak negatively about the king or the royal family.

Buddha and monks

Most Thais are Buddhist, and most Thai men are monks at some time in their life. They wear the traditional saffron robes and do not eat after midday. To give to a monk is said to 'make merit'. They will not thank you, as your merit is thanks enough. Women may not touch monks.

Buddha images (statues) are sacred. Do not touch them on their head, or with your feet. In temples, do not wear shorts, and women should keep their shoulders covered.

Most businesses (and hotels) have either a 'spirit house' outside, or a niche on an inside wall. They give flowers, food and water to the spirits every day. Thais are very superstitious and they believe that sprits of the deceased live in their houses. The daily offerings are to make peace with the spirits.

The Wai

The traditional Thai greeting is the wai – hands together as if in prayer, and bow slightly. It does not mean 'hello', but is a mark of respect, so in general do not wai back, especially to doormen etc. However, Thais are used to farangs (that's us) waiing back, so it's not a big error. Best to smile back politely. It's OK to wai to monks, and the king, should you meet him.

Insider tip: You may hear Thais call us 'falangs' also. They often pronounce the letter 'r' as an 'l'.

No losing face

For Thais it is important to keep their temper and not lose face. So if your hotel reservation is lost, the best thing to do is to smile politely and insist that they find it. Do not get angry as that is much frowned upon, and will not get you anywhere.

Age is respected, 'No' is not

Thais respect people their elders – that is why Thais may ask 'how old are you?" (No need to provide an answer). They also may sometimes ask 'how much do you earn?' That is not impolite in Thailand, and the correct answer is 'not enough!' Thais will generally avoid responding to a question with 'no', so if you ask a question like 'Do you have any children?', they may answer 'not yet'. You ask, "Do you like beer?", they answer 'A little." That means no.

Thai food and bottled water

Thai food in Thailand is a bit different from the American and British version of Thai food except in big hotels – it tends to be hotter. Be cautious about eating from roadside stalls. Drink only bottled water in Thailand, even to brush your teeth. Thais do not use chopsticks when eating, but a spoon and fork. Except that they use chopsticks for noodle soup. Go figure.

Missionaries

Christian missionaries have worked in Thailand for many years. They have had some success in the northern part of the country, and Chiang Mai sees many Christian churches, particularly in Watgate, east of the Ping River. However, Christianity is a very small part of Thai culture, and most of the population are Buddhist.

Thai Values

Buddhism shapes Thai values to a large extent, but the concept of fun, or *sanuk*, is very important to Thais also. You will also hear Thais say *'mai pen rai'*, which means 'that's OK', or 'it doesn't matter'. Thais are usually a relaxed and easygoing people.

4: Chiang Mai Hotels

Hotel guide price ranges:
$ 2,000 - 5,000 baht ($50 - $140,   £37 - £92)
$$ 5,000 – 10,000 baht ($140 - $280, £92 - £185)
$$$ 10,000 – 15,000 baht ($280 - $420, £185 - £277)
$$$$ 15,000 – 20,000 baht ($420 - $560, £277 - £370)

There are backpacker hostels and guest houses in Chiang Mai, but we do not cover them in this book. Our hotel price ranges start at about $50 a night. Lonely Planet, for example, covers less expensive hostels.

Budget Hotels

Dusit Princess ($) Ideally situated in the center of town, near the night bazaar. Used to be known as the 'Royal Princess', now remodeled with a new name.   Three restaurants, including 'Jasmine' Chinese. Very good buffet breakfast is included. Swimming pool. Many bars and restaurants within easy walking distance (and Starbucks). Tuk-tuks and taxis are available outside the front   door.   112   Chang   Klan   Rd. *Dusit.com/dusitprincess/chiangmai*

Insider tip: Deluxe rooms are bigger than the regular Superior room, and located on the 2-7 floors.   The swimming pool is on the second floor.

B2 ($) Located on Charoenrat Rd in Watgate, a new hotel built in 2015. Room rates start at 1,800 baht a night. 053 244-426. *B2hotel.com*

Insider tip: The Dusit Princess (located in the center of town) and the B2 (located in busy Watkate) represent the best value for the budget traveler.

Ninetynine The Gallery Hotel ($). A modern boutique hotel at a budget price. 99 Inthawarot Rd. 053 326-338. *99thegalleryhotel.com*

Chiang Mai Plaza Hotel ($) Centrally located between the night bazaar and the river. Swimming pool, fitness center, spa and travel desk. ($) 92 Sridonchai Road.

Insider tip: Almost next door to The Whole Earth, one of the best Indian and vegetarian restaurants in town. French bakery down the street.

Hollanda Montri Guesthouse ($) Family style guesthouse on the river, with a tropical garden. Ten minutes from town. Sometimes they have live music at weekends. Airconditioned rooms. 365 Charoenrat Road. 053 242-450.

Baan Orapin ($) A boutique B&B with just six rooms in a beautiful old Thai house. In Watkate over the road from the Ping River. 150 Charoenrat Rd.

Pornping Tower ($) An older central hotel with 'Bubbles', a popular disco. Close to the river and many restaurants. 46-48 Charoenprathet Road. 053 270-099.

Insider tip: *The newer Tower Wing is away from the disco noise.*

Boutique Hotels

Rachamankha ($$) In the old town on a small soi (small lane off the main road), next to Wat Phra Singh, the city's most famous temple. 25 rooms and suites. Colonial charm with rooms around courtyards. Pool and library. Excellent restaurant, in shady courtyard with stage for live music, or inside. Small up-market bar. 6 Rachamankha Soi 9, Phra Singh. 053-904-111. *Rachamankha.com*

Insider tip: Some rooms are small. Notice the cut glass decanters of complimentary drinks for readers in the library.

Sala Lanna ($$) On the banks of the Ping River in Watkate. 16 room boutique hotel, most with river views. Rooftop bar. Sala Thai restaurant on the river. Good area for art galleries and walking to restaurants etc. Limited parking. 49 Charoenrat Rd, Wat Gate. 053-242-588. *Salaresorts.com*

[25]

Ping Nakara ($$$) White colonial hotel with graceful gingerbread architecture, close to town and on the river. 19 rooms, pool and spa. Restaurant in garden. Library. 135/9 Charoen Prathet Rd. 053-252-999. *Pingnakara.com*

Raming Lodge ($) Lanna Thai style boutique hotel between the night bazaar and the city. Restaurant & swimming pool. 17-19 Loi Kroh Road, Chang Klan. 053-271-177.

The Rim Resort Chiang Mai ($$) In the old city by the moat. Centered on an old colonial Lanna house. 36 guest rooms. Swimming pool, restaurant, bars. Tropical garden. Room butler service. 51/2 Arrak Rd. 053 253-666. *Therimchiangmai.com*

Insider tips: A bit far from the main attractions for easy walking, but you can get a tuk-tuk outside the door. The hotel provides a mini bus to the night bazaar every evening. Very small pool, and pool-view rooms can be noisy.

Baan Huen Phen ($) A family run boutique hotel with character and style. Pool. Close to Sunday Walking Street. 117/1 Rachamankha Rd. 053 281-100. *Baanhuenphen.com*

Mid-Range Hotels

D2 ($$) Owned and managed by the Dusit Group, a large modern hotel very close to the night bazaar. Pool, restaurant, gym and bar. Dance party nights. Walk to shops, bars and restaurants. 100 Chang Klan Road. 053 399-999.

Shangri-La Chiang Mai ($$) Large hotel on the edge of town with rooms decorated in contemporary northern Thai style. Good Sunday brunch. Restaurants (including upscale Chinese restaurant), pool and spa. 89/8 Chang Klan Rd. 053 253-888. *Shangri-la.com/chiangmai*

Meridien Chiang Mai ($$)

Modern hotel with a huge marble-floored lobby. Next to the night bazaar. Restaurants and bars - good Italian restaurant on the first floor. (One floor up) Sunday brunch. Latitude 18 dance club, with dance classes. 108 Chang Klan Rd. 053 253-666. *Lemeridienchiangmai.com*

Insider tip: If you have a car or motorbike, there is good free restaurant parking in the hotel basement.

Up-Market Hotels

Chiang Mai has a good selection of up-market hotels, both in town and outside of town. Here are the best of them:

Four Seasons Resort ($$$$) 30 minutes from Chiang Mai near the bustling little town of Mae Rim, though the hotel transportation uses a leafy back road, so you wouldn't know it. Rooms in Thai villas overlooking the gardens and rice fields. Terraces restaurant by the pool for western food and Sala Mae Rim near the lobby for excellent Thai food. Patio bar. Big spa and pool. Good cooking school. Several shops at Lan Sai Village. Mae Rim / Samoeng Old Road, Mae Rim. 053-298-181. *Fourseasons.com*

Insider tips: The rice terraces rooms are in sets of four to a villa, two upstairs and two downstairs. Choose the upstairs rooms for the best view. The footpaths between the rooms are uneven small stone slabs, difficult for ladies with high heels. So request a buggy to take you to your room. There is a free van service to the center of town five times a day.

Dhara Dhevi Chiang Mai ($$$$) About 15 minutes from town just off the Sankampaeng road, and difficult to find the first time. Looks like a temple. Lanna style Thai villas and colonial suites in 60 acres of lush grounds. Le Grand Lanna Thai restaurant, Farang Ses, expensive French, and Fujian, Chinese dim sum in the shops nearby. Coffee shop in Kad Dhara is good if you are just stopping by. Cooking school. Pools and spa. 51/4 M1 Chiang Mai / Sankampaeng Road. 053-888-888. *Dharadhevi.com*

Insider tip: Used to be the Mandarin Oriental, Chiang Mai, and that name is still used by many locals. It's a long walk on an uneven cobbled drive from the parking lot — request a buggy. Drinks in the Horn Bar are expensive, and the many antlers on the wall are an odd touch.

137 Pillars House ($$$) Not far from the river in Watkate. 30 modern suites, surrounding an original teak villa which now houses the restaurants and the bar. The main building was built as the headquarters of The Borneo Company in 1856. A peaceful hideaway from town. Pool and spa. Afternoon tea. 2 Soi 1, Nawatgate Rd. 053-247-788. *137pillarshouse.com*

Insider tip: It's an easy walk to the many riverside restaurant / bars nearby, particularly The Riverside and The Good View. But no real bar at the hotel.

Anantara ($$$) On the banks of the Ping River. 52 guest rooms and 32 suites. The main building used to be the British Consulate, and now houses 'The Service 1921' and 'The Restaurant'. Good western, Thai and Indian menus. Afternoon tea. Wine tastings. Cooking school. Big pool and spa. Easy walk to the center of town. 123 Charoen Prathet Rd. 053-247-788. *Anantara.com*

Insider tips: Used to be called 'The Chedi' and many locals still call it that. There is a new '1921' restaurant with a spy theme and a good bar.   In the main restaurant, you can request a table on the patio beside the river.

When the building was the British Consulate in 1903 a statue of Queen Victoria was erected in the grounds. It has now been moved to the Foreign Cemetery, next to the Gymkhana Club.

5: Getting About

Walking

Chiang Mai is an excellent city for walking – if you can avoid the potholes and motorbikes on the sidewalks! The central area of town is quite small and easy to navigate. However sidewalks, which are not always present, can be blocked by parked motorbikes so be prepared to walk in the street.

Walking tips

- Get a copy of the Nancy Chandler Chiang Mai map (from most hotels and all bookstores), or download a copy of the Chiang Mai central area map, especially the walled city and the area between the city walls and the Ping River.

- It can get hot! Wear a hat.

- Bring a bottle of water.

- Wear comfortable walking shoes. Dress appropriately for temple visits, covering the arms and legs.

- Don't plan to do too much in one day.

Insider tip: There are pedestrian crossings, but if they have no red light to stop traffic, use them at your own risk! Traffic will rarely stop. Best to wait for a break in the traffic and cross quickly.

Tuk Tuks and Songthaews

Tuk tuks are brightly colored three-wheel taxis, which you will find outside many hotels and restaurants, and popular places like the Night Bazaar. Few tuk tuk drivers speak English, but they do know the names of the popular tourist destinations. Ask the fare before you get in, and be prepared to bargain. Most tuk tuk fares are in the 50 to 100 baht range. ($2 - $3).

You may occasionally see a 'tuk tuk parade' of ten or twelve tuk tuks, sometimes with a flashing police escort, in the early evening on their way to a restaurant with a group of tourists.

Insider tip: Tuk tuk drivers are paid bonuses for taking tourists to certain stores and they may try to divert you. They might even claim that your destination is closed and they know a better place. 'Temple closed today!' Always insist on going where you want to go. If necessary, find another tuk tuk.

Songthaews (song taws) are the colored pickups (usually red in the center of town) that cost 20 baht per person flat rate. Flag down a Songthaew and tell the driver where you are going.

If he says 'yes', get into the back of the pickup. He may go to other places on the way, and pick up other riders. When he reaches your destination, ring the bell, get out, and pay him 20 baht.

If he says 'no', he is not going your way, so step aside and find another Songthaew. Look for a red Songthaew if you are in the city. White, green and blue ones go outside the city.

Taxi Meters

Yellow cabs are particularly popular at shopping malls and the airport. These have a meter to show the fare. They are more expensive than a tuk tuk, but more comfortable and have metered fares. If the meter is not working, which often happens, make sure to negotiate the fare before setting off.

Taxi Service Call Center: 053 241-955

Private taxis

Private taxis are regular cars or minibuses that can be booked by arrangement, usually by phone. Private taxi drivers often wait for business outside popular hotels. The Dusit Princess on Chang Klan Road is a good example. The name of the company may be written on the side of the vehicle.

Private taxi: Mr Wirat Nabunrat, English spoken. 088 806-0353 062 950-3069

Private taxi: English spoken. 053 140-890   053 922-128.

Private taxi: Mr Chai. 081 617-1928

Segway Tours

Segway Gibbon. Including a local guide and instruction. 084 614-4004. *Segwaygibbon.com*

Bicycle rental

Bicycles as a form of transportation have been around in Chiang Mai for decades, particularly as bicycle rickshaws. (There are still a few about). Recently, cycling has become increasingly popular with locals, expats and tourists. Many hotels and guest houses provide bikes to guests for free. There are also many bike rental shops offering reasonable rates. You may be asked for a deposit or to leave your passport. A passport copy or a passport card, is usually accepted. Make sure to get a bike lock.

Insider tip: Many streets are not well lit so avoid riding at night. Streets are busiest between 7-9am and 5-7pm, so avoid those times if possible.

SpiceRoads is one of the best bike rental shops, with a fleet that includes mountain, hybrid and road bikes. Child bikes and child seats are also available. Helmets are provided for 50 baht. Bikes can be picked up at 34 Nimmanhaemin, Soi 7.

Two Revolutions. Klai Muk soi 4. 090 465-6123.

Jacky Bike Shop. 12/7 Nimmanhaeimin Soi 13. 053 225-278.

There are also bike racks in many areas of town owned by **Bike@Chiangmai**. (Tha Phae gate, Three Kings monument, Nawarat Bridge, Wat Phra Singh, etc). Open 8am – 8pm. Rates are 20 baht for the first hour, 60 baht for 4-5 hours, and 100 baht over that. A special card is needed to rent a bike and there is a first time fee for the card of 120 baht. To get the card call 085 139-2410.

Motorbike and scooter rental

There are many places to rent a scooter or motorbike in Chiang Mai. There are motorbike hire shops, and most resorts, backpacker hostels and monthly accommodation places either have their own scooters or can quickly obtain one with a phone call.

It's best to rent from a place that speaks English. Some places take credit cards, but not all. So best to have cash.

Renting a scooter

There are three main types of scooter:

- Fully automatic – no gears

- Semi automatic – gears but no clutch

- Manual – gears and clutch

The fully automatic is the easiest to ride. Most scooters come in the 110cc, 115cc and 125cc size. The Honda Dream / Wave is a good choice, a 110 – 125cc four-stroke single cylinder scooter.

Before taking the scooter to a complete visual check and photograph any scrapes or damage on your phone. Select the newest bike that they have. Take the bike for a ride and check the brakes and acceleration. Make sure that you have the number of the bike rental shop in case of an accident or a flat tire.

You will be asked to leave a security deposit or leave your passport as security. It is best to pay the deposit, and not leave your passport, as you should always carry your passport with you. You can leave a passport copy with them. Do opt for insurance, but make sure that it is full coverage – some insurance cover requires you to pay for any damage. Remember to drive on the left!

Motorbike rental

Kawasaki and Honda now manufacture bigger bikes in Thailand, in the 250, 500 and 650cc range. Be aware of your limitations – it is not necessary to ride a big bike to enjoy the scenery.

Insider tip: Thailand can be a dangerous country to drive in if you are not cautious. Make sure that your travel insurance included motorbike driving – some do not.

Motorcycle rental shops

Mr Mechanic. 4 Soi 5, Moon Muang Rd. 053 214-708

One of Chiang Mai's largest rental fleets. Kawasaki, Honda, Suzuki.

Mr Beer. 2 Rajwithee Rd. 053 418-236

Honda Wave, Honda Dream, Kawasaki, Yamaha

Pop. 3 Kotchasarn Rd. 053 276-660

Many bikes available, including Honda PCX-150, Kawasaki Ninja,Suzuki

Tony's Big Bikes. 17 Ratchamankha Rd. 053 207-124. *Chiangmai-Motorcycle-Rental.com*

Large selection of bikes of different sizes, including BMW, Kawasaki, Yamaha, Honda, Suzuki

Insider tip: *Tony's Big Bikes is British owned and has a knowledgeable staff.*

Helmet laws

It is mandatory to wear a helmet if you are riding a motorbike or scooter. This is quite strictly enforced and there are police checkpoints where they will give you a ticket if you are not wearing a helmet.

Insider tip: The police checkpoints are often at the same places. One spot often used for a checkpoint is the city side of the Nawarat Bridge.

Car rental

You can rent a car from many places in Chiang Mai, but if you are arriving and departing from the airport, the airport car rental offices are the most convenient, though they may cost more. Here are the four main airport car rental locations.

Avis

Avis has a well-staffed office at the airport and many cars. (The Avis office which was at the Royal Princess hotel for many years has now closed, now that the hotel is the Dusit Princess.) 02 251-1131 *AvisThailand.com*

Hertz

Hertz is the second major car rental office at the airport, though they usually have fewer cars than Avis. 02 266-4666. *HertzThailand.com*

Budget 053 207-871

Sixt Rent a Car 053 279-000

Off-Airport Car Rental

Thai Rent A Car 053 904-188

North Wheels 053 874-478

Pop Car Rent 053 276-014

Neu Speed Car Rent 053 270-702

Journey Co Ltd. 053 206-487

National Car Rent 053 210-118

Insider tip: If you are given a choice of car, choose one with a red license plate. Brand new cars have red license plates!

Driving in Thailand

Thai urban roads are busy and there are bikes and scooters everywhere. The traffic takes a little getting used to, and of course they drive on the left. Local drivers behave as if red stop lights are 'just a suggestion'! Traffic lights can take several minutes to change in your favor, so when the light turns red it is not unusual to see 3, 4 or 5 cars and motorbikes go through on red. Cars and bikes often turn in front of you, even if you have the right of way. So drive defensively and be aware that Thai drivers seem to make their own rules.

For example: You are turning right from the right turn lane. It is not unusual to see tuk-tuks or motorbikes pull up alongside, on the right, in the middle of the road. Hopefully they will be turning right with you, but no, they may well be going straight ahead. So watch out!

Parking

Thai drivers invariably back into parking lot spaces because it's easier to pull out in the limited space available. Also, cars blocking other cars in a busy lot is normal in Thailand. The cars are left in neutral, and can be easily pushed out of the way, sometimes with the help of the guard, if there is one.

Red and white check curbs mean 'no parking' and the rule is tightly enforced. If you park there, you may get clamped, and receive a ticket on your windscreen.

Insider tip: Should you get clamped, you need to go to the police station on Praisani street (near the river, between the Nawarat Bridge and the Warorot Market), present the ticket and pay a fine. They will radio a motorcycle officer to remove the clamp, usually by the time that you get back to your car.

The only motorway in the Chiang Mai area is the 'Super Highway', and the main roads are well maintained by the Ministry of Transport. Most main roads between cities have four lanes and a central divider.

Insider tip: If you see an accident (most likely a tumble from a motorbike or scooter), it's tempting to stop and see if all is OK. That is not a good idea. In the confusion following an accident, particularly if the police are called, any wealthy western person (farang) on the scene (that is you) is likely to be blamed for the accident. The assumption is that you have plenty of money to pay for the damage! All of this takes place in Thai which you probably don't understand. So unless you are involved, leave road accidents to Thai motorists and go on your way.

Thai Insider: Chiang Mai

6: Things to do in Chiang Mai

Elephant camps

In Thailand, elephants were used in warfare and logging for hundreds of years. Nowadays their numbers are in decline, and elephant camps make these fine animals available for tourists. There is a close relationship between the elephant and his or her mahout (who takes daily care of the elephant) – often for life. There are many elephant camps in the Chiang Mai area. Here are some of the most popular.

Maesa Elephant Camp

The best known elephant camp in the area. About 40 elephants live at the camp, including some baby elephants. There are three shows every day, where elephants play soccer, build a log wall, burst balloons with darts and paint pictures, which can be purchased after the show. Elephant rides are also available. The two person ride lasts about half an hour, with riders on a wooden seat on the back of the elephant. The elephants also steal and replace hats from tourists and accept tips – 20 baht is suggested. Using their trunk they take the 20 baht note from your hand and carefully hand it to the mahout on their back.

The office (to book elephant rides) is at 119/9 Tapae Road, in Chiang Mai. 053 206-247. *Maesaelephantcamp.com.* The elephant camp itself is on the Mae Rim to Samoeng Rd, a few miles west of Mae Rim. About 40 minutes from town.

Patara Elephant Farm

This is an all-day visit in which your care for 'your own elephant', so is very different from the Maesa Elephant Camp. You feed, clean, and ride your elephant, sitting on its neck like a mahout, not on an elephant seat. You will be invited to inspect the dung to make sure that your elephant is healthy! (It's pretty harmless vegetable matter). At the end of your day you will be given a CD of photos of your visit. It's a way from town but the price includes hotel pick-up. About 6,000 baht per person for the day ($200). Book early as it tends to fill up several weeks ahead – best to use the web site before you get to Chiang Mai.

299/22 Mae Hea, Chiang Mai. 081 992-2551 *Pataraelephantfarm.com*

Elephant Nature Park

This camp offers opportunities for volunteers to take part in elephant care and training, often for a week or month at a time. The cost is about 12,000 baht a week ($400) including accommodation and meals. Day visits are also available for about 3,000 baht ($90) which includes lunch.

209/2 Sriodom Chai Rd, Chiang Mai. 053 818-754. *Elephantnaturepark.org*

Save Elephant Foundation. Dedicated to protecting Asian elephants. Discover elephants in their natural environment. 1 Rachamankha Rd, Phrasing. (200 meters from Thapae Gate). 053 272-855 *Saveelephant.org.*

Chai Lai Orchid

Stay with elephants at a mountain eco-resort, raft down the river and plunge into the fresh mountain water pool. Hike to hilltribe villages. *ChaiLaiOrchid.com*

City walks

There are two fairly short city walks that are of particular interest, with good restaurants, bars and shopping. These are described in detail in the 'Two or three days in Chiang Mai' chapter.

Temples

Some tips for visiting temples

- Dress in appropriate clothing, covering your arms and legs.

- Before entering a temple, turn off your mobile phone, remove your hat and shoes.

- When greeting a monk, do so with a 'wai'. Place your palms together at chest level, as if in prayer. Bow slightly. The monk will not wai back.

- Be prepared to make a donation in one of the offering boxes. 20 or 100 baht is appropriate.

Doi Suthep

Wat Phra That Doi Suthep is the best known temple in Chiang Mai. If you plan to visit just one temple, make it this one. It's on a big hill a few miles outside of town.

Legend has it that a monk called Sumanathera found a bone relic believed to be from the Buddha. He put the relic on a white elephant, which traveled far until he reached Doi Suthep, then trumpeted loudly and died. The temple was constructed on that spot starting in 1386.

There is a great gold-plated chedi (a stupa or dome shaped structure) in the upper level, built in the 14th to 16th century. It is traditional to circle the chedi three

[51]

times in a clockwise direction. Pilgrims can strike rows of bells as they circle the chedi.

The views from the upper level extend over the whole of Chiang Mai. Hours: 8am – 5pm.

Insider tip: To reach the temple there are over 300 stairs, but you can take a funicular to the top for a small fee. It is not well signposted but it is on the right of the main entrance.

Wat Phra Singh

Wat Phra Singh is located at the end of Rachadamnoen Rd, in the old walled city of Chiang Mai.

The temple houses an important Buddha statue, Pra Buddha Singh, which gives the temple its name.

Insider tip: It is alleged that the statue was stolen in 1922 and that the present statue is a copy.

The temple complex was begun in 1345. In the Burmese rule period in the 15th and 16th centuries it fell into disrepair, until it was restored in 1782. Further restoration took place in the 1920s and 2002.

Wat Chedi Luang

The original Chedi (42 meters high) was the tallest structure in Chiang Mai for over 500 years. It was restored in the 1990s, and is found behind the present-day temple.

All Thai temples have donation boxes. You can write your name and a wish on an envelope, put your donation inside, and place it in a big bowl high on a table.

Monk Chat at Temple of the Great Stupa

The Great Stupa includes a jade replica of the Emerald Buddha.

An informal Monk Chat is held here every day from 9am until 6pm. The chats are held at outside tables on the north side of the temple compound. You can ask the monks questions about Buddhism or their life. Out of respect, sit lower than the monk and do not point your feet at him. Don't interrupt when the monk is speaking.

It is customary to offer a donation – 100 baht is appropriate.

Wat Umong

This wat is different – a temple in a forest cave! A little way past Nimmanhaemin Road on Suthep Road. Turn left on soi 4. Chedi and underground chapels. Words of wisdom tacked onto the trees. Lectures in English most Sundays at 3pm.

Insider tip: **'What's What in a Wat'**, by Carol Stratton is a good book about Buddhist temples in general. Published by Silkworm books in Chiang Mai. *Silkwormbooks.com*

Boat trips on the Ping River

Mae Ping River Cruise. Choose from a long tail boat, traditional teak rice barge or a large boat for groups. Sit down and relax over fresh fruit or herb juice. Includes a stop at Thai Farmer's House. 8.30am – 5.30pm. Boat departs every hour. 13 Charoenprathet Rd. 053 274-822. Email: Maepingrivercruise@hotmail.com. *Maepingrivercruise.com*

Rice Barge Boat Trip. Next to Wawee Coffee in Watkate, near the Nawarat bridge. Daily departures at 9am, 11am, 1pm, 3pm and 5pm. 350 baht per person. A leisurely boat trip down the river with a stop for refreshments at a Thai farmer's house. 053 274-822.

Golf, Tennis, Mountain Bikes, Ziplining

Look for descriptions of these and other activities in the 'Sports and Fitness' chapter.

Cooking Schools

Baan Thai Cookery School. You can learn how to cook real Thai food in a traditional Thai setting. Skilled and friendly teachers in a fun atmosphere. Day or evening classes. In Thai, Baan Thai means Thai home, and they look forward to sharing Thai cooking and culture with you. Located off Walking Street a few blocks from Tha Pae Gate. 11 Rachdamnern Rd, soi 5. 053 357-339. *Cookinthai.com.*

7: Chiang Mai Restaurants

There are three roads of particular interest for bars and restaurants.

Charoenrat Rd. On the east side of the river, in Watkate between the Nawarat Bridge and the Nakorn Ping Bridge. Many good restaurants and bars, particularly The Riverside and The Good View.

Loi Kroh Rd. Traffic runs one way, from the city walls to the river. The end near the city walls has many busy bars (some with female hostesses). Chez Marco is also in this area.

Nimmanhaemin Rd. North east of the city walls, near the University. Many bars and restaurants. Some are on Nimmanhaemin itself (like Sahara and Salad Concepts) but many more are on the Sois, the small side street. The odd numbered Sois on the west of Nimmanhaemin (Soi 1 – 13) have the most bars and restaurants. Sometimes the address gets abbreviated like this: Nimman soi 9.

Insider tip: There is a good Starbucks with a patio at the corner of Nimmanhaemin and soi 9 (the *coffee soi*)

The Nancy Chandler map of Chiang Mai (available at bookstores and at *Amazon.com*) has most popular restaurants marked, and is an invaluable aid to finding your way around the town.

Ordering

Most restaurants cater to western people and have menus in both Thai and English. The servers will usually understand limited English, so try to speak slowly and clearly. If they have difficulty understanding your order, it can be helpful to point to the item on the menu, where it will also be written in Thai. Thai customers will often say 'one' after ordering an item, or your server may ask 'one?' after you order.

Wine and Drinks

Alcoholic drinks and a choice of soft drinks are available in most restaurants. Because of taxes, wine can be much more expensive in Thailand than at home. When there are wines by the glass often only one red and one white will be offered. Beer comes in two sizes, 'large' and 'small'. The water in restaurants is safe to drink.

How was your meal?

Your waiter or waitress may ask you, "And what about your dinner?" Sometimes they ask this when you are just starting your meal. The correct response is *"Di maak"* (very good), or *"Aroi maak"* (very delicious).

Insider tip: Thais will always respond with *Di maak* or *Aroi maak,* no matter what they think of the meal. To say anything less would not be polite. But you can show your true feelings by how much enthusiasm (or lack of it) you put into using one of these two phrases.

Tipping

In Thailand it is not necessary to leave a 'percentage' tip in most restaurants. In very good restaurants or a nice hotel you may still want to leave 10-15%, but in most restaurants Thais will tip 20 or 100 baht. Some more expensive restaurants (often in hotels) will already have a service charge of 10% added. In that case it is usual to leave 100 baht as a little extra.

Paying your bill

To ask for your bill, ask for *Gep taang* (followed by *krub* if you are male, or *kaa* if you are female) in Thai, or 'check bill', in English (which Thais will pronounce as 'check bin'), which will be understood. They will present the bill, you will hand over your cash or credit card, and they will take it to the cash desk. There is always a central cash desk where bills are processed and change made. The server will then bring your credit card or change back to the table. Be patient because this can take several minutes.

Budget / Casual

The Riverside - On the banks of the Ping River, one of the most popular casual restaurants in Chiang Mai, with extensive Thai and western menus. Full every night, so best to book. Mostly English speaking staff. Their less busy Craft Beer Factory (a second restaurant with imported craft beers) is just over the road, with a nice garden and waterfall. Both restaurants have soft jazz early and a rock band starting at 9.30pm. Easy walk from town via the Nawarat Bridge. 9 Charoenrat Rd, Watkate. 053 243-239. *Theriversidechiangmai.com*

Insider tips: The restaurant only reserves 30% of tables, so you can go and wait if you don't get a reservation. Request a table on the balcony if you want a good river view. The Craft Beer Factory tends to be less busy, so you can usually get in if the Riverside is full. Tuk-tuks wait outside to take you back to your hotel.

The Good View - Large venue next door to The Riverside but with a much more Thai clientele. On the river. Good Thai and western food, and a nonstop live band. Can get very crowded and noisy. Also '**Sip**' bar next door under same ownership, which has a DJ late at night. Tuk-tuks outside. 3 Charoenrat Rd, Watkate. 053 302-764. *Goodview.co.th*

Deck 1 – Modern riverfront restaurant next to The Riverside (on the other side to the Good View). Inside and outside dining. Parking opposite. Charoenrat Rd, Watkate. Buffet breakfast. Open daily 7am – midnight. 053 302-788.

Chez Marco - On Loi Kroh Road, known locally as the 'bar street'. A big expat favorite. Sizzling steaks! Mediterranean cuisine. Vegetarian dishes available. Kids menu. Lively patio or air-conditioned inside. 15/7 Loi Kroh Road. 053 207-032.

Sahara - On busy Nimmanhaemin road, a Moroccan restaurant and wine bar. Upstairs bar patio with low tables. Middle eastern, Thai and western food. 59/9 Nimmanhaemin Rd. 053 222-088. *Saharathai.com*

Giorgio's - Old fashioned Italian restaurant close to town. Good wine list and friendly staff. Just off Chang

Klan Rd. They also own Da Antonio, nearby. 2/6 Pracha Samphan Rd. 053 271-866. *Giorgiochiangmai.com*

Da Antonio – Busy Italian restaurant with BBQ. Just off Chang Klan Rd. 11/1 Charoenprathet 12 Rd. 053 233-160. *Giorgiochangmai.com*

Hinlay Curry House – Serving up fabulous Indian, Thai and Burmese curries for many years. Vegetarian options. In a small garden in Watkate. Credit cards accepted. 10am – 10pm. 8/1 Na Wat Gate Soi 1. 053 242-621

Chang Puak Night Market - Great local food, including Khao Kha Moo, praised by TV travel host Anthony Bordain. Manee Nopparact Rd, Chang Puak Gate. 5pm – 2am daily.

Art Café - Opposite Tha Pae Gate near the moat, air-conditioned. Varied menu includes western and Thai, even Mexican. Tha Phae at Kotchasan. 053 206-365. *Artcafechiangmai.com*

Rustic & Blue – Original food, local and homegrown, with an inventive combination of ingredients. Popular with expats. Indoor and outdoor dining. 8.30am – 5pm. Nimmanhaemin soi 7. 053 216-420.

The Whole Earth – Indian, Thai and vegetarian cuisines. Upstairs in an old Thai house with polished wooden floors – diners remove their shoes downstairs. 11am – 10pm. 88 Sridonchai Rd. 053 282-463.

Insider tip: Opinions differ as to whether the restaurant at Anantara or The Whole Earth has the best Indian food in town. Both are very good - The Whole Earth is more traditional and Anantara is more modern.

Le Spice - On a small soi just off the night bazaar, owned by an Indian family. Indian and Thai dishes. 31 Soi 6, Charoen Prathet. 053 234-4983.

Korea House - Korean restaurant serving traditional barbecue & grilled meat. Chang Moi Rd. 053 251-982. *Café.naver.com/koreahouses*

Miguel's Café - Yes, there is a good Mexican restaurant in Chiang Mai! Located just off the moat, probably the best Mexican food in town. Eat inside or on the patio. Good margaritas, and pitchers. 106/1 Chaiyaphum Rd. 053 874-148.

Insider tip: You often see Thai people enjoying 'foreign' restaurants, like Italian or French, but rarely at Mexican restaurants! There is a small parking lot on the left just past Miguels. Or get a tuk tuk outside the door.

W by Wanlamun - Well hidden away down a small soi, a Thai restaurant in a white house with seating in the garden. It also serves pastries and coffee. Closed Monday. Chang Moi Soi 2. Another location at Central Festival mall. 053 232-328. *Wanlamun.com*

Sushi Box - Over 70 sushi items to choose from, all prepared fresh. 5pm to 10pm every day. 28 Ratwitthu Rd. *Facebook: Sushiboxcm*

The Duke's - Steaks, ribs, seafood, burgers and pizza. It uses only imported Australian beef for its steaks. When you've had enough of Thai food and are in the mood for good American ribs or burgers, head over to The Duke's! Ping River branch (near the Watgate side of the Iron Bridge) 49/4-5 Chiang Mai – Lamphun Rd, Watgate. Also located at Promenada mall, Night Bazaar and Maya Mall. 053 249-231 *Wherestheduke.com.*

Insider tip: For delivery from The Duke's or many other restaurants in town, call Meals on Wheels 4U on 084 608-6661 or *Mealsonwheels4u.com.* All restaurant menus are available online, including The Dukes, Butter is Better, Paradise Pizza, Miguels Real Mexican Food, La Fontana and The River Market.

The River Market - Owned by The Dukes and situated on the Night Bazaar side of the Iron Bridge. The Thai-Burmese colonial looking building was built with reclaimed wood just a few years ago. Good Thai and western food, with no MSG. Live music some nights. Various clubs like the Rotary Club and the Chiang Mai Expat Club meet here. Cooking school. Charoen Prathet Rd. (On the river near the Iron Bridge) 11am – 11pm. 053 234-493 *Therivermarket.com*

Insider tip: If you walk across the Iron Bridge, don't miss the 'Bus Bar' on the city side of the bridge – an old bus converted to a bar!

The Pub - Located near Nimmahaemin road in a garden, this 45 year old pub has all the old-fashioned ambiance of an English bar. Fish and chips. Roast lamb and roast beef Sunday lunch. English breakfast. Sports on TV and live music outside sometimes. Also **Cubano**, Chiang Mai's first Cuban restaurant, in the garden. Rum marinated pork chop, classic chuuasco. 189 Huay Kaew Rd. 053 211-550. *Thepubchiangmai.com*

Mix - Innovative Thai, Chinese, European and Japanese cuisine. For the young, hip and thirsty set, this is a place to be seen. Molecular mixology cocktails that use liquid nitrogen to change liquor into gelato. Winner of many awards. Nimmanhaemin soi 1. Also Central Festival and Promenada mall. 081 472-9664. Facebook*: mixcnx*

Italics – A new take on Italian and Thai dining, at the small five star Akyra hotel. Locally sourced high quality ingredients. Good wine and champagne list. 22/2 Nimmanhaemin Rd soi 9. 053 216-219

Wine Connection - Deli and Bistro in a wine shop, in the Central Festival shopping mall. 053 288-841 *Wineconnection.co.th*

Insider tip: There is also a Wine Connection at the Promenada Mall. Because Wine Connection is a shop, the restaurant in Central Festival mall has to comply with Thai liquor buying laws. You can only buy wine (or have wine with a meal) between the hours of 11am to 2pm, and then after 5pm.

La Fourchette – A taste of Paris in the heart of Chiang Mai - a charming small French restaurant. Open Monday – Saturday 5pm – 10pm. Reservations suggested. 162/2 Thanon Phrapoklao. Opposite Wat Chedi Luang. 089 758-5604 (English). *Restaurant-la-fourchette.com*

Ginger & Kafe - On the inside of the moat. Interesting Thai and western menus, coffee and cake. Charming décor - velvet sofas and antiques. Full bar. English speaking. Open 10am – 11pm. Also Ginger home / lifestyle / clothing shop next door. 199 Moonmuang Rd. 053 419-011 *Thehousethailand.com*

Upscale / Splurge

Favola - On the first floor (one floor up) of the Meridien hotel, this restaurant serves great Italian food and pizza. Open kitchen and large glass wine cellar. Sunday brunch. Good wine list. Free parking in the basement. Le Meridien. 108 Chang Klan Rd. 053 253-299. *Lemeridienhotelchinagmai.com*

Insider tip: Best to book, but you can only book after 5pm. Can be quiet early evening. Request a table by the window for a good view of the night bazaar.

Le Crystal - Purpose-built glass-walled riverfront formal French restaurant 20 minutes out of town. Riverfront terrace. Great wine list. Dinner only. 18.00 hrs to 22.30hrs. 74/2 Paton Rd. 053 872-890. Email:info@lecrystalrestaurant.com. *Lecrystalrestaurant.com*

Insider tip: Booking is essential. They will pick you up from your hotel.

Le Coq D'Or - Upscale French cuisine. The first five star restaurant to open in Chiang Mai, in 1973. Many awards including Thailand Tatler best restaurant many years running. Specialities include white truffle soup. Manager: Narongchai. 11 Kohklang Rd. 053 141-555 Facebook:LeCoqDorChiangMai.

David's Kitchen at 909 - Owned by David & Thanyarat Gordon and Arthit Dissuront ('Chef O'), David will escort you to your table, which will be reserved with a personal greeting card. Air-conditioned main restaurant. Chef O is formerly from the Dhara Dhevi hotel, and his specialities include fois gras with sweet mango chutney, pan seared tuna, braised lamb shank, veal tenderloin, and a spectacular sticky toffee pudding for desert. Whisky & cigar room. 113 Bamrungrad Rd, Watgate. (Opposite the British Council.) 091 068-1744. Email: Info@DavidsKitchenat 909.com. *Davidskitchenat909.com*

Insider tip: They moved January 2016 from a location far outside of town to the new location in Watkate. If you have the 90/9 Moo 3 Sansipuur Rd address, that is the old location, so do not go there!

Farang Ses - At the Dhara Dhevi, a formal French restaurant with chandeliers, teak ceiling and white tablecloths. Chef Carlos Gaudencio brings Paris-trained classical French cuisine to this elegant restaurant. Great wine list. Expensive, reservations required. 20 minutes out of town. 51/4 Th Sankampaeng. 053 888-888. *Dharadhevi.com*

Tengoku de Cuisine – Fine Japanese dining across from the Dhara Dhevi hotel, 20 minutes out of town. Menu includes Wagyu beef, eggplant with miso sauce. Good service. Reservations preferred. 55/8 Soi wat buak krok luang. 053 851-133.

The Restaurant - Located at the Anantara hotel, this riverside restaurant has an Indian and western menu. Very good Indian food. Afternoon tea. Jazz trio some nights. In the same hotel is '**The Service 1921'**, named after the building's first use as the British Consulate in 1921. The downstairs 1921 bar and upstairs restaurant have a 'secret service spy' theme of that era, with menus in manila envelopes, and spy pictures on the walls. Thai, Chinese and Vietnam cuisine on one 'secret' menu. Anantara. 123 Charoen Prathet Rd. 053 253-385. *Anantara.com*

Insider tip: Avoid stepping into the clear-water pond as they lead you through the restaurant lobby! Some inside tables can accommodate large parties. You can request a patio table by the river.

Piccolo Roma - Located directly opposite the Anantara hotel, one of the best Italian restaurants in town. Opened in 1991. Chef / owner Angelo Faro is much in evidence, and will usually take your order. On the wall are pictures of many famous people who have been to the restaurant. Free pickup from your hotel. 144 Charoenprathet Rd. 053 820-297. *Piccoloromapalace.com*

White Lotus - Located a few miles outside of town in Mae Rim. Offers authentic Vietnamese cuisine. 398/8 Palm Spa Village (Moo Ban Impress), Mae Rim. (On road 1260 linking Mae Rim to Mae Jo). 081 753-0358 Email: WhiteLotusRestaurantMaeRim@gmail.com

Ruen Tamarind – In the Tamarind Village Hotel. Innovative southern Thai food. Lovely hotel setting and lively guitarist at night. 50/1 Rajdamnoen Rd. (Sunday walking street). 053 418-896.

Rachamankha - In the Rachamankha Hotel, within the old city walls. Elegant dining inside or in the courtyard. Thai, Myanmar, Lanna and European cuisines. 6 Rachamankha 9, Phra Singh. 053 904-111. Email: Sales@Rachamankha.com *Rachamankha.com*.

L'Elephant - Romantic tiny restaurant in a shop filled with knickknacks. Good wine list from temperature controlled wine cellar. Private room available for groups. Definitely need to book. 7 Sirimangalajam Soi 11. Closed on Thursdays. 097 970-8947.

Terraces - At the Four Seasons in Mae Rim. About 30 minutes drive from the city. Distant green mountains and lush paddy fields. Thai and International menus. Impeccable Four Seasons service. *Fourseasons.com/chiangmai/dining/restaurants/terraces*

Vegetarian

Anchan Vegetarian - Delicious vegetarian meals prepared from fresh organic ingredients. Smoothies, oolong tea and wine. Nimmahaemin Road, opposite Soi 13. 083 581-1689.

My Home Café & Vegetarian - Features clean white décor, a green space of shady trees, and the sounds of running water from a fountain. Vegetarian and vegan foods. Thanawan Village Soi 11. Closed Sunday. 081 027-0050 Facebook: *My Home Café Vegetarian*

Insider tip: Look for the yellow flags on food stalls. This means that they serve vegetarian food only. There is a two week vegetarian festival in October.

Breakfast

Bake & Bite - Two great breakfast locations with a full menu, lots of bread, bagels, rolls, cakes cookies and brownies – all freshly made! Nimmanhaemin Soi 9 (down from Starbucks) Closed Wednesday and Kaewnawarat Soi 3/2 (near to Watkate) Closed Friday. 053 249-689.

Insider tip: Some locals mishear the name and call these two restaurants 'Bacon Bite'!

Butter is Better - Decorated with 1940 Hollywood movie posters. Pastries, breads, soups & casseroles. They use only genuine butter in pastries. Easy walk from town and the night bazaar. 189 Chang Klan Rd, and two other locations.   Cash   only.   053   820-761. *Butterisbetterbakery.com*

Insider tip: Owner and pie maker Dao says, "The ingredients have to be coddled from beginning to end. Except for cream, which sometimes needs to be whipped!"

Smoothie Blues – Very good all day breakfast in the busy Nimmanhaemin area. Big menu. Has an outside area. 32/8 Nimmanhaemin soi 6. 053 227-038

Cat Cafes

Yes, Chiang Mai has several cafes where you can play with your furry friends while you drink your coffee. Signs will tell you not to wake the cats if they are sleeping!

Maewmoth Cat Café - 10am – 8pm. Closed Tuesday. 100/2 Soi Wat Umong, off Suthep Rd. 086 672-9802 *maewmoth.com*

Catmosphere - 10am – 9pm. Closed Monday. Panna Project, 223/5 Huay Kaew Rd. 092 273-1011 Facebook: *Catmospherecafe*

Love Cats Café - Noon – 8pm. Closed Monday. The Harbour, above Catnip Wine Bar, 16/1 Huay Kaew Rd. Facebook: *Lovecatshousechiangmai.*

Coffee & Cake

Woo - Café and art gallery in Watkate. Nice mismatched wooden tables and flowers. Good drinks and light meals. Outdoor patio seating or indoor air conditioned. Lifestyle shop next door. 80 Charoenrat Rd, Watkate. 052 003-717. *Woochiangmai.com*

Wawee Coffee - A Thai-owned coffee shop that is all over town. The one in Watkate, by the Nawarat bridge has a nice riverside patio.

Starbucks - All over town, with the same coffee menu that you have at home. Good snacks and desserts.

Dhara Dhevi cake shop - 20 minutes out of town, in the small shopping area of the Dhara Dhevi hotel. Good cakes and pastries. 51/4 M1 Chiang Mai – Sankampaeng Rd. 053 888-888.

Love at First Bite - Cakes and coffee in a garden, down a small soi on the Watkate side of the Nawarat bridge. Homebakes pies and cakes. Chiang Mai – Lamphun Rd M1. 053 242-731.

Lucky Bunny Café - A café in which you can interact with 35 playful bunny rabbits! Times are 11am, 2pm and 4pm each day (closed Thursdays) and you need to book. Baan Nonnipa Village, Mae Jo. 085 195-5465 *Facebook: Lucky Bunny Café Restaurant*

Nakara Jardin - A café in a riverside garden behind the Ping Nakara Hotel. Pastries, lunch and afternoon tea. Open 11am – 7pm. Closed Wednesday. Charoenprathet Rd. 053 818-977.

Raming Tea House - Organic tea and coffee in an elegant colonial teak house in a nice garden setting. Celadon pottery. 158 Thapae Rd. Open 8.30am – 6pm. 053 234-518. *Ramingtea.com*

Insider tip: A white building, five minutes walk from the Night Bazaar street. You can take tea in the very nice garden behind the store.

Rist8to Coffee – Said by locals to be the best coffee in Chiang Mai. On Nimmanhaemin road between soi 1 and 3. Another branch at Central Festival. Open 7.08am – 6.08pm. 15/3 Nimmanhaemin Rd. 053 215-278

8: Chiang Mai Bars & Clubs

There are several hundred bars and clubs in Chiang Mai, some catering mainly to Thais, but most with an international clientele. Johnny Walker Black Label Scotch whisky is very popular with Thais. It is said that more Johnny Walker Black is consumed in Thailand than they make in the distillery in Scotland, so go figure! If you are a 'regular' at many popular bars (The Riverside, for example) you can buy a bottle of your favorite drink and leave it at the bar with your name on it. Then next time, ask for your bottle and pay only for ice and mixers.

Most places will keep your bottle for up to three months. Some bars employ 'whisky girls' in short dresses, ready to pour Johnny Walker Black Label for their Thai customers.

British readers may be used to ordering beer by the pint or half pint. In Thailand, beer comes in 'large' or 'small' sizes, and the two main domestic makes are Singha and Chang. So you might ask for 'One Singha small', for example.

Bars

UN Irish Pub -Live sports on TV. Popular with expats. Always packed when a big match is on. Soccer, cricket, rugby, tennis, golf. Irish breakfast. 24-234/1 Ratwithi Rd. 053 214-554.

The Writer's Club & Wine Bar – Popular with local writers on Friday nights when they have a 'writer's night'. Good wine selection. A convenient stopping off point for the Sunday Walking Street market. Open 12 noon to midnight. 141/3 Ratchadamnoen Road (Walking Street) near Wat Chedi Luang. 053 814-187.

The Pub - Located near Nimmahaemin road in a garden, this 45 year old pub has all the old-fashioned ambiance of an English bar. Monday night general knowledge quiz night, all welcome. Also **Cubano**, a new Cuban restaurant in the garden. 189 Huai Kaew Rd. 053 211-550. *Thepubchiangmai.com*

The Riverside - On the banks of the Ping river, one of the most popular casual bars in Chiang Mai. Mostly English speaking staff. Their less busy Craft Beer Factory bar & restaurant is just over the road, with a nice garden and waterfall. Both bars have soft jazz early and a rock band starting at 9.30pm. Easy walk from town via the Nawarat bridge. 9 Charoenrat Rd. 053 243-239. *Theriversidechiangmai.com*

Insider tips: This is one of the most popular bars in town. The Riverside and the Craft Beer Factory over the road (same owners) are full every night. Tuk-tuks wait outside to take you back to your hotel.

The Good View - Large venue next door to The Riverside but with a much more Thai clientele. On the river. Good Thai and western food, and a nonstop live band. Can get very crowded. Tuk-tuks outside. 3 Charoenrat Rd. 053 302-764. *Goodview.co.th.* Also **Sip Bar**, a tiny place next door, with a DJ.

Beer Republic – Imported and Thai beer. 28 Nimmanhaemin Soi 11. 5pm – midnight. 081 531-4765.

O'Malley's Bar – Air conditioned Irish pub near the Night Bazaar. Good Irish breakfast. 9am – 11pm. 149 14-15 Chang Klan Rd, Amusarn Market. 053 271-921.

The Red Lion – Long-established English pub near the Night Bazaar (on a side road). Indoor and outdoor areas. 9.30am – 11.30pm. 123 Loi Kroh Rd. 053 818-847.

Number 1 Bar – Belgian and craft beers. In a small soi off Loi Kroh Road, in the bars area. 12 noon – 2am. Soi 1, Loi Kroh Rd. 053 206-724.

Chiangmai Saloon – American style burger and steakhouse with good drinks. 80/1 Loi Kroh Rd (near the Night Bazaar) 080 675-2169 and 30 Rachwithi Rd (near the moat) 081 930-2212.

Monkey Club - This long-established club very popular with Thais was being rebuilt as we went to press. Nimmanhaemin Soi 9. 053 226-9978.

Hotel Bars

The Service 1921 – Anantara Chiang Mai Resort's colonial spy hideaway. This one has a real bar that you can sit at, and a British Secret Service spy theme. Anantara. 123 Charoen Prathet Rd. 053 253-385

The Horn Bar - At the Dhara Dhevi hotel, 20 minutes outside of town. Chiang Mai – Sankampaeng Rd. 053 888-888.

Insider tip: Ask for a golf cart ride to and from the parking lot as the driveway is cobbled and uneven – a difficult walk in the dark. The drinks are the most expensive in town.

Mix Bar at the D2 – Close to the Night Bazaar, an open long bar extending into the modern hotel lobby. 100 Chang Klan Rd. 053 999-999.

Rise Bar – at the new Akyra small five star hotel. The bar is on the roof, with an extensive wine and champagne list. Sunset happy hour 5.30pm – 6.30pm. Friday night DJs 9pm – 11pm. 22/2 Nimmanhaemin Rd soi 9. 053 216-219. *Theakyra.com*

Live Music Bars

Papa Rock - Thursday evening open mike jam session from 9.30pm. Sunday afternoons too. Can be quiet. Off the Hang Dong road, first ring road. 086 729-2039

Boy Blues Bar - Popular music bar on the first floor of the Night Bazaar. Live music every night. Monday night jam night for local musicians (mostly western).

Insider tip: If you go on a Monday night, try to arrive between 8pm and 9pm to get a seat before the music jam starts. There will be no seats later!

North Gate Jazz Co-op – Live jazz club near the moat and the Chiang Puak gate. Jam night on Tuesdays. Open 7pm – midnight, music starts around 9pm. Opposite Chiang Puak gate – the north gate of the city.

Rasta Café – Popular outdoor bar located next to the Iron bridge over the Ping River. Features live reggae and ska nightly, and a sprinkling of jazz and rock. Open 7.30pm to midnight. 73/10 Charoen Prathet Rd. 081 690-1577.

The Brasserie – Features Chiang Mai rock legend Took, though he doesn't start playing until 11pm. On the outer moat road close to Miguel's.

Roots Rock Reggae – Busy most nights with Thais and backpackers listening to reggae and ska music. Small lane off Ratwithi Rd. 9pm – 1.15am. 053 418-424.

Escudo Supper Club – Open 7pm – 1am. Late night dancing. Can be very quiet early evening. 15 Charoenrat Rd, Watkate. 086 118-5556. *Escudosupperclub.com*

Gay Bars

Ram Bar – Chill out gay bar near the Ping River, opposite the Diamond Riverside Hotel. Open 6pm – 12am. 085 034-5607

Soho Bar – Gay owned and managed and belongs to the Soho Guesthouse. Full bar from 5pm. 20/3 Huay Kaew Rd. 053 404-175

Glass Onion – Sophisticated wine bar popular with local gays. 61 Nimmanhaemin Rd. 053 218-479.

Warm Up Café – Opposite the Glass Onion. Bar, restaurant and disco. Open 6pm – 1am. 40 Nimmanhaemin Rd. 053 400-676.

Secrets Bar – 48 Chroenprathet Rd. 081 531-5566.

Insider Tip: Dreaded Ned is the most popular gay website in Thailand, with hotels and guesthouses, bars and pubs, restaurants, saunas, etc. Good Chiang Mai coverage. *Dreadedned.com.*

Ladyboy Bars

Ladyboys are often seen in Thailand. They are young boys who dress up and act like girls, often very realistically. It is said that in Thailand there are three sexes – male, female and ladyboys!

The Shamrock – Said to be the best ladyboy bar in town. Boxing Stadium Complex. 96-98 Loi Kroh Rd.

Marina Bar – Another cheerful ladyboy bar in the Boxing Stadium Complex. Loi Kroh Rd.

Go-Go Bars

Like every tourist area in Thailand, Chiang Mai has its share of Go-Go bars and girly bars. These are mostly centered around Loi Kroh Road – the 'bar street'. There is also a popular Go-Go bar, **The Foxy Lady**, behind the D2 hotel in the night market area.

A 'mini Tokyo' exists near the Anantara hotel, with Karaoke bars exclusively for Japanese and Korean clientele. You can't get in unless you are one of these nationalities.

Insider tip: Some karaoke bars are tourist traps in which you buy drinks for your hostesses and then are presented with a very inflated bar bill when it's time to leave. The charge includes drinks, hand towels and ice, and the expensive privilege of talking to your hostesses!

At the night market end of Loi Kroh road is the Chiang Mai entertainment center (also known as the Boxing Stadium Complex) , with many girly bars, a couple of Go-Go bars, and some Ladyboy bars.

9: Shopping in Chiang Mai

Shopping in Chiang Mai ranges from street markets to modern shopping malls. Top buys are lacquer, silk, Celadon, tribal artifacts, ceramics and silver jewelry. Bargaining is the norm at market stalls but not in shops or shopping malls.

Markets

Night Bazaar

The Night Bazaar is not to be missed. Located on Chang Klan Rd in the eastern part of town (between the moat and the river), the market consists of hundreds of stalls open between 5pm and midnight. The stalls sell handicrafts, copy watches and leather goods, food, clothing, spices, Thai silk, and silver items. Hillside women walk about selling 'croaking wooden frogs'. Plan to offer half to two thirds of the price first quoted, and end up paying around two thirds to three quarters of that price.

Insider tip: If you are the first customer of a stall, the stallholder will be eager to make a sale, as that will be 'lucky' for him or her, and they will wave your money across the goods in the stall for good luck. You can get a good deal if you are the first customer of the evening.

Walking Street Sunday Market

Starting at the Tha Phae gate and extending west a couple of miles along Ratchadamnoen Rd (Walking Street), the Walking Street Market is open only on Sunday evening. It differs from the Night Bazaar in that the items are mostly handicrafts and food (no fake watches and bags etc). The street can get very crowded. There are many musicians (some of them blind) sitting in the center of the street as the crowds pass by on either side.

Amulet Market

One of Chiang Mai's most interesting bazaars. The market features thousands of Buddhist amulets, some of which are antique. Prices range from 20 baht to over 10 million baht. Every Thursday from 7am to 2pm north of the old city off the Superhighway behind the Tesco Superstore.

Wararot Market

On the banks of the Ping River beside the new pedestrian bridge. Best visited in the morning before the heat of the day. The market sells fruits and vegetables, flowers (both for the temple and for the home), fabrics, beads, clothing, electronics and plastics.

Insider tip: The Nancy Chandler Map of Chiang Mai has a detailed map of Wararot Market, showing what is for sale in each area.

Bo Sang Handicraft Village

On the outskirts of town on the Chiangmai - Sankamphaeng road (Highway 1006). The village is well known for its hand-made colorful paper umbrellas, which can make great decorations.

The Colour Factory / Elephant Parade House.

A fun activity for the whole family. Paint a model resin elephant! The workshop costs 1,000 baht for a 15cm elephant or 600 baht for a 10cm elephant. 20% of Elephant Parade profits are donated to the Asian Elephant Foundation, which supports projects across Asia for elephant conservation. Open 10am – 8pm. 154-156 Charoenrat Rd, Watkate. 053 246-448. *Email: Info@elephantparadehouse.com*

Bookstores

There are many good used and new bookstores in town. Chang Moi Kao Road near Tha Phae Gate is an area which contains several used bookstores.

Gecko Books. 2/6 Chang Moi Kao Road. 053 874-066. *Geckobooks.net*

Backstreet Books. 2/8 Chang Moi Kao Road. 053 874-143. *Facebook: Backstreetchiangmai.bookshop*

The Booksmith. 11 Nimmanhaemin Road, Soi 3. 080 441-*0888 Facebook: Thebooksmithbookshop*

On the Road. 38/1 Ratwitthi Road.

Shaman Books. Kotchasan Soi 1. 053 235-652

Book Republic. 34/12 Moo 5 Irrigation Canal Rd. 053 617-825 *Facebook:BookRepublicChiangMai*

Lost Books. 34/4 Ratchamankha Road.

Asia Books. Mostly in shopping malls.

Celadon

The story of Celadon goes back more than two thousand years. Celadon is known as the ancestor of the pottery family and takes its name from the elegant glaze developed by master potters in northern China. It is now very popular in Chiang Mai.

Siam Celadon. Same building as the Raming Tea House. 158 Thapae Rd. 053 331-958.

Baan Celadon. For two decades, Baan Celadon has been producing a wide range of Celadon home wares. Large showroom a little way out of town. They will ship. 7 Moo 3, Chiang Mai Sankampaeng Rd. 053 338-288 *Baanceladon.com*

Shopping Centers & Malls

There are many good shopping malls in Chiang Mai. These are the best known.

Insider tip: When you pay in a department store, don't expect to immediately get your change in return. They will take your money or credit card and walk to the cash desk with it, which may be some distance away. They will return with the receipt and change several minutes later.

Central Airport Plaza

For years the largest mall in town, on five floors. A big Robinsons department store. (Thai owned, not the American Robinsons.) A unique 'Northern Village' for high quality local handicrafts. Open weekdays 11am – 10pm, weekends 9.30am – 10pm.

Insider tip: This mall is known by many locals as 'Robinsons'.

Central Festival

A very large mall on the east side of town, which has in some respects taken over from the Central Airport Plaza mall. Many English stores including Marks & Spencer. Wine Connection. Open 10am 10pm.

Insider tip: Parking is in a multi-story parking structure with the second floor (walls painted pink) being reserved as a 'ladies floor'.

Promenada Resort Mall

About 20 minutes out of town, and can be quiet – other malls are closer to town. Restaurant options include Dukes, Ragu Rustico Italian, Matsusaka, Wine Connection, Mix Promenada and Black Canyon Coffee.

They have occasional music events outside. Open 10am – 9pm.

Maya Lifestyle Shopping Center

A smaller mall, near to Nimmanhaemin Rd. Very modern and western-like. Good movie theater on 5th floor, with English language movies. Good branch of Rimping supermarket in the basement. Open 10am – 10pm.

Tech Plazas

There are several tech plazas in Chiang Mai, selling computer software and hardware, printers, phones etc.

The closest one to the center of town is **Pantip Plaza**, on Chang Klan Rd, close to the Dusit Princess Hotel.

10: Sports & Fitness

A visitor to Chiang Mai may be surprised at the array of sports and fitness facilities there are to choose from.

Partly as a result of the construction that occurred when Chiang Mai became the first non-capital city to host the prestigious South East Asian games in 1995, the area features some world class sports facilities, including the Gymkhana, Thailand's oldest sports club.

In most cases, participation in the activity of your choice can be easily and quickly arranged, even at short notice. If you are staying at a hotel, the concierge always is a good place to get prices, locations, reservations, tee times, and other pertinent information.

Golf

Compared to most of the rest of the world, greens fees are inexpensive in Chiang Mai, the equivalent of $15 or less at most courses. It's always best to call ahead and reserve a tee time. While those included are not all the golf courses in the area, they are a representative list and among the most interesting. The prices listed are subject to change.

Insider tip: Greens fees Monday through Friday are less than on weekends.

Chiang Mai Green Valley Country Club – Twenty minutes north of the city on Route 107 (telephone: 053 298220), the 18-hole course features flat fairways that slope toward the Ping River. Greens fees: weekdays 1440 baht; weekend 1,920 baht. *summitgreenvalley.com*

Royal Chiang Mai Golf Club – Thirty minutes north of Chiang Mai toward Phrao (telephone: 053 84 9301), the 7,200 yard pat 72 layout was designed by famed British golf course architect Peter Thompson. Greens fees: weekdays 1,400 baht; weekends 1,800 baht. *royalchiangmai.com*

Lanna Golf Club – On Chotana Road less than two miles north of the Old City Road (telephone: 053 221911), it's a heavily wooded 27-hole course with great views of Doi Suthep Mountain. Greens fees: weekdays 1,200 baht; weekends 1,400 baht.

Insider tip: If you didn't bring your clubs, don't worry. Virtually all courses rent clubs and even golf shoes for a small fee.

Gymkhana Golf Course & Sports Club – The oldest golf club in Thailand was established in 1898 and was a favorite of British writer Somerset Maugham during his visits to what was then called Siam. It's the only golf course within the inner city (on Lamphun Road) and the atmosphere harkens back to an earlier time. For example, golfers must wear collared shirts. The club also offers tennis and cricket. The course is only nine holes, so to get in 18 holes you have to go around twice, but at only 600 baht it may be the best deal in the area. The fairways are narrow and heavily wooded. The clubhouse restaurant and bar are perfect for a lazy lunch. 053 241-035. *chiengmaigymkhana.com*

Insider tip: If you've never played with a caddy, Thailand is a good place to indulge yourself. It costs only 200 baht to hire a caddy at most clubs, plus a tip – the caddies live off the tips.

Chiang Mai Highlands Golf and Spa Resort. Nominated for 'Best Golf Resort in Asia' 2015 Asian Golf Awards. 053 261-354. *Chiangmaihighlands.com*

Mae Jo Golf Resort & Spa. Located just 20 minutes away from Chiang Mai city. 053 354-431. Email: info@maejogolfclub.com. *Maejogolfclub.com.*

Tennis

Tennis is a popular sport in Chiang Mai. Many hotels have their own courts or have an arrangement with a nearby tennis club, so it's best to check with the concierge to see what's available. Racquets can always be rented and sometimes even tennis shoes. For an additional small fee, hitting partners are easy to arrange, too.

Insider tip: For night play, there usually is a small additional charge for electricity, although some clubs simply charge a higher per hour fee at night.

[93]

Chiang Mai Land Public Tennis Courts – With three well-maintained courts, the fee is 100 baht per hour during the day and 140 baht per hour at night. Hours are 8 a.m. to 9 p.m. Especially during the summer heat, evening play is quite popular and the courts can be crowded. The club also features a swimming pool and light meals are served in the club house. Telephone: 053 27 2821. Located at 90/1 Chiang Mai-Lampang Superhighway.

The 700 Year Stadium – With 12 regular courts and one stadium court for exhibitions, this club has the largest number of tennis courts in Chiang Mai, part of a large sports complex that was built for the Southeast Asian Games in the mid-1990s. The fee is 60 baht per hour and the hours are 6 a.m. to 9 p.m. Telephone: 053 11 2052. Address: 284 Moo 3 Chiang Mai-Fang Road.

Anantasiri Tennis Courts – A favorite place for locals, it's usually easy to pick up a match at this public court facility, located across from the National Museum on the Chiang Mai-Lampang Superhighway. 50 baht per hour.

Muay Thai

This combat sport is arguably the most popular spectator sport in Thailand, especially with the rise in popularity of mixed martial arts throughout the world. Muay Thai combines fists, elbows, knees and shins for striking and defense. Its history as a martial art can be traced to the 16th century. Reportedly, the King of Thailand is a fan. In Chiang Mai, it can be seen at three venues.

Loi Kroh Boxing Stadium - Located at 28 Loi Krok Road in the Chiang Mai Entertainment Complex near the night market, be aware that sometimes the bouts are really advanced sparring sessions between rival schools. Fights are held three or four nights a week with eight fights per night and it's easy to find posters advertising the fights all over the old city. Admission is 400 baht for regular seating and 600 baht for VIP seating. Telephone: 089-852-6947

Insider tip: Virtually surrounded by a variety of "girlie bars" and "lady boy bars," it's not as family friendly as other venues. Between bouts, sometimes lady boys will dance in the ring.

Thaphae Boxing Stadium - Located on Moonmuang Road behind the Thaphae Gate and next to the Top North Hotel, this facility attracts a large crowd of mostly foreigners. Admission is 500 baht, with a higher price for VIP seats close to the ring. Usually eight fights per night, including matches with foreign fighters. There are several bars scattered around the arena. 086 187- 7655 *thaphaestadium.com*

Insider Tip: This is the place to go if you've never seen the sport and want to sit in relative comfort with hundreds of fellow tourists. There's a narrow alley entrance and a tout on the sidewalk will show you in.

Kalare Boxing Stadium – Located right behind the night bizarre with fights Wednesday, Friday and Saturday starting usually at 9:30 p.m. and lasting about four hours. This venue probably offers the best fights in town, usually featuring fiercely dedicated Thai boxers intent on moving up in the rankings. Admission is 400 baht for regular seating and 600 baht for VIP.

Insider tip: You will see a lot of gambling at these venues. It's easy to get caught up in the atmosphere but don't waste your money. A few of the bouts may be only enhanced exhibitions. Just enjoy the experience.

Gyms and Fitness

Absolute Bootcamp Fitness. 7 day and weekend bootcamps. #3 Soi 13, Nimmanheamin Rd. 082 889-2377

Crossfit Chiang Mai. Coaching and personal training in a group session. Constantly varied, high intensity, functional fitness. Challenging and fun conditioning and strength training classes for all levels of fitness. 48/1 Chiang Mai / Lampang Rd (Superhighway). Near Wat Jed Yod, 5 minutes from Nimmanhaemin Road. 094 610-1665.

Yoga

Yoga Bright. 72 yoga classes per month. Sky Fly aerial fitness class. Pilates. Bathrooms, dressing rooms and lockers. Green Plus Mall. 053 851-545. *Yogabrightchiangmai.com*

Healing Retreat

Chotikam Retreat. A resort specializing in Ayurvedic Theory, healing by nature, a technique dating back over 5,000 years. One day program is 5,000 baht. Mae Rim. 086 919-3131 (English).

Pilates

Pilates Plus. All training is done one-on-one with a certified trainer and top-of-the-line equipment. Two locations. Punna Place, 2nd floor, Nimmanhaemin Soi 6. 053 400-301. Meechok Plaza, 3rd floor. Clock Tower. 053 430-231 *Pilatesplus-studio.com*

Ice Skating

The Central Festival mall has a new ice skating rink. Prices are 160 baht per hour for children, 200 baht for adults or 500 baht for a whole day. Skating classes available. 023 542-134. *Central festival.co.th/chiangmai.*

Bicycle Touring and Mountain Biking

There are many legitimate companies offering unique bicycle tours of the region, including options ranging from family friendly to extreme.

Biking in the hills out of town, you get a different perspective on the area, a slower, and closer, look at nature, sights and people. There are many agencies that offer day, overnight and multiple night trips, but one of the most highly regarded is **Contact Travel** (420/3 Chang Klan Road) 053 204-664. *Activethailand.com.* Day trips start at 2,100B.

Just west of Chiang Mai is the beautiful Doi Suthep National Park, where **Chiang Mai Biking** runs daily downhill trips and cross-country rides, plus many other day trip and overnight excursions. Most day trips start at about 2000 baht. 081-024-7406. *Mountainbikingchiangmai.com.*

Bike & Kayak Adventure organize tours in the Chiang Mai area, including the Mae Ngat Rice Valley. Tours start at the Ban Den Temple Complex. Office at 1 Samlan Rd. 053 814-207. *Mountainbikingchiangmai.com*

[98]

Ziplining

Does the idea of flying from tree to tree through a 1,500 year old rain forest while suspended by cable appeal to you?

If so, you might enjoy ziplining, an increasingly popular activity around the world. In the Chiang Mai area, there are two major companies based in the mountains east of Chiang Mai that offer jungle ziplining adventures:

Flight of the Gibbon (*treetopasia.com* 053 010-660) where tours are 3,999 baht ($115). Over 5km of ziplines with the world's longest single zipline. In a treetop canopy with skybridges to view the flora and fauna. Wild gibbons. Traditional tribal museums and Northern culture museum.

Jungle Flight, where fees for a more barebones experience start at 2,150 baht. ($61) (*Jungleflightchiangmai.com* 053-208-666). Both organizations will pick you up at your hotel, or wherever you happen to be staying.

Insider tip: Keep in mind that it's about a 90 minute bus ride to both sites, not including stops at other hotels to pick up customers. Add that to the ziplining itself and it becomes an all-day experience, even if it's touted as only a half day.

Gun Shooting Ranges

Mae Rim Shooting Range. Located on the Mae Rim – Samoeng Rd, it provides a safe and attractive open air environment with both paper and metal silhouette targets. Thirteen shooting stalls accommodate pistols up to 45 caliber and rifles up to 22 caliber. 817 Moo q, Mae Rim-Samoeng Rd. 081 595-7113. *Maerimshootingrange.com*

Shooting Club, 3rd Development Battalion. Many types of quality guns with qualified instructors providing safe instruction. 8.30 am to 5.30 pm. Chiang Mai – Mae Rim Road. 053 112-095. *Shootingclubcm.com.*

The Fox BB Gun. Fully equipped 2-rai (large) battle field. Friendly and helpful staff. Amateurs are welcome. 63/1 Chiang Mai – Sankampaeng Rd. 081 671-0990 (for English). *Thefoxbbgun.com*

Segway Tours

Segway Gibbon. Looking for a new way to see Chiang Mai? A Segway Gibbon tour includes a guide with local knowledge to show you the basics of riding a Segway. 084 614-4004. *Segwaygibbon.com*

11: Massage and Personal Care

Massage and Spas

The art of massage is popular in Chiang Mai and certainly less expensive than the United States or Europe. Your hotel may be able to arrange for a massage, either in the hotel spa or in your room. There are also many spas available around the city. These are some of the best known:

Oasis spa. This is the best known spa in Chiang Mai with four locations each with the same phone number. Choose an individual treatment and spend an hour or an afternoon. There is a complete menu of treatment and therapies: scrub, wrap, facials, reflexology and body massage. 10am – 10pm. 053 920-111. Email: res@oasisspa.net. *Oasisspa.net.*

Oasis Oriental Secret Spa. Their newest location. 35 Rattannkosin Rd, Watkate.

Oasis Spa Chiang Mai. 102 Sirimuanglajan Rd, Suthep.

Oasis Spa Lanna Near to Wat Pra Singh and walking street. 4 Samlan Rd, Prasing.

Oasis Spa Baan Saen Doi. A small spa with five treatment rooms. 199/135 Moo 3, Chonoratan Rd, Mae Hia.

Other spas:

Lanna Come Spa. A spa in the northern Thai style. 84 Sridonchai Rd. 053 274-377. Email: info@lannacomespa.com. *Lannacomespa.com*

Peak Spa. Ayurvedic massage, hot stones massage, traditional Thai massage, L'Oreal hair salon. Free transportation. 187/13 Chang Klan Rd. 053 818-869. Email: Contact@peak-spa.com *Peak-spa.com.*

Cheeva Spa. Thai and Swedish massage. Lanna style. Free transportation. Open 10am – 9pm. 053 405-129. Email: Contact@Cheevaspa.com. *Cheevaspa.com.*

The Spa at the Four Seasons. A worthy destination in itself. On the grounds of the Beautiful Four Seasons Hotel in Mae Rim, half an hour from town. Mae Rim – Samoeng Old Rd. 9am – 11pm. 053 298-181. *Fourseasons.com.*

The Dhevi Spa. Lanna spa at the Dhara Dhevi hotel, 20 minutes out of town. Heated marble massage beds, Vichy showers, hydrotherapy baths. 51/4 M.1. Chiang Mai – Sankampaeng Rd. 053 888-888. *Dharadhevi.com.*

Rarinjinda Wellness Spa. Extensive treatment menu. Yoga classes and its own hotel and restaurant. Next to the Riverside restaurant. 14 Charoenrat Rd, Watkate. 053 247-000. *Rarinjinda.com.*

The Artist Spa. Relaxing spa experience for men and women. 8/3 Nimmanhaemin Rd. 053 218-875 (English speaking) *Theartistsspa.com*

Kiyora Spa. An experienced team of therapists providing premium service and expertise. Book online and save 50%. 26/1 Chang Moi Rd, Soi 2. 053 003-268. *Kiyoraspa.com*

Medical and Personal Services

Chiang Mai (like Bangkok) is an excellent place to get elective medical care. See the note below on medical tourism.

Dentists

Grace Dental Clinic. American-trained dentists work in this bright dental surgery, the best known for western visitors to Chiang Mai. 45 Nimmanhaemin Soi 11. 9am – 8.30pm. 053 894-568. *Gracedentalclinic.com.*

Heart Dental Clinic. Implants, teeth whitening. 389/23-24 Moo 2, San Phi Suea. 053 110-827 Email: Heartdentalcliniccm@gmail.com

House of Dental Care. Class One Complex. 85 Moo 1, Huaykaew Rd. 053 217-845. Email: Classonedentistry@gmail.com. *Classonedentist.com*

Skin Care

Pure Natural Skincare Center. Herbal spa treatments and Guasa, an ancient Chinese skin treatment that uses a wooden stick to scrape the skin to aid in detoxification. Open daily 10am – 8pm. Curve Mall, Chang Klan Rd. 053 272-096

Chat – Peera Clinic. Founded by two dermatologists, Chat – Peera Clinic is the place to go for problem skin that needs professional assistance. Laser equipment to cure skin pigmentation issues. Open Monday – Saturday 11am – 8pm. 42/2 Nimmanhaemin Rd. 053 223-089.

Pharmacies

There are several Boots the Chemists, and more specialized pharmacies. One of the best known is **Peera Pharmacy**, on Walking Street (Ratchadamnoen St), which stocks a broad range of medications, many of which need a prescription back home. In Thailand you can get most medications (except opioids) without a prescription.

Opticians

There are many storefront opticians in town offering eye tests and new glasses made on the spot in less than an hour.

Vision Center. Accurate eye tests and good service. English spoken. Close to the UN Irish Pub. 18/2 Ratwithi Rd. 053 418-336.

Hair Stylists

Absolute Hair Studio. Unisex. 29/3 Huay Kaew Rd. 053 894-492

New York, New York. Stylist Vera Ramasute lived in New York for many years. Avada products. 13/2 Soi 13 Nimmanhaemin Rd. 053 215-199 *Newyorknewyorkhairstudio.com*

Hospitals

There are many hospitals in Chiang Mai. Ram Hospital and Bangkok Chiang Mai Hospital are the best known for westerners. For a full list see the 'Useful Information' chapter.

Chiang Mai Ram Hospital 053 224-861

Bangkok Hospital Chiang Mai 052 089-817

Medical Tourism

The cost of medical care in Thailand is one quarter to one third the cost of similar care in the USA or Europe. Hospitals are modern and the standard of care is very good. Many people come to Thailand for elective medical care – medical tourism. It is often said that you can pay for the flights, your medical care and a stay in a nice hotel at a total cost that is still far below what you would pay just for medical treatment back home.

12: Thai Food

Everyone knows that Thai food can be hot and spicy, but it's probably more spicy (hotter) in Thailand than you may be used to at home. If you want it less hot, ask for it *mai pet* (not hot).

Despite what you sometimes see on TV, Thais do not eat with chopsticks but use a spoon and fork. Chopsticks are used only for Chinese food and noodle dishes.

Napkins are rarely seen in Thailand. Unless you are in an upscale restaurant there may be a jug on the table with tiny napkins the size of a square of toilet paper. (Or sometimes, an actual roll of toilet paper!)

The dishes in Thailand usually come to the table as they are prepared, not all at once. Most are served family style – the dishes are placed in the middle of the table for everyone to share. Thais often do not order all the dishes at one time, but one at a time, ordering a new dish as they finish the one before.

Place a small heap of rice onto your plate, help yourself to small portions from dishes on the table and place them beside your rice. It's polite to take only a little at a time. Eat with the fork in your left hand to push the food onto your spoon.

If you are a regular in a restaurant you can usually order a bottle of whisky, rum, gin, vodka, etc, and they will keep it with your name on it. Then when you return to the restaurant you can ask for your bottle, and you need only pay for mixers and ice.

Thai cuisine is different in various parts of Thailand. It is often more spicy in the south and northeast, and milder in the midsection, including Chiang Mai. Sticky rice (*khao nio*), *som tam* and *khao soy* are also popular in Chiang Mai.

Meat is usually chicken (*gai*), pork (*moo*) or beef (*neua*). Also available is seafood (*talay*), shrimp (*goong*) and duck (*ped*). Popular dishes include pork fried with garlic and black pepper, sweet and sour pork, and Chiang Mai sausage.

Noodles are also popular and come in two types, made from wheat flour (*ba mee*) and made from rice flour (*kuay tiaw*). A popular dish is *paad thai* (pan fried rice noodles with shrimp, peanuts and bean sprouts with a fried egg on top.)

"Pad Thai is one of the most commonly recognized dishes in Thai cuisine. It is a balance of sweet, savory, salty and sour. At Eat & Drink Restaurant we like to use shrimps and wrap this dish in a thin egg omelet." Mrs Kongsi Phutatpet, chef at East & Drink Restaurant, Chiang Mai.

Some Dishes from a Chiang Mai Restaurant Menu

- Royal Thai style chicken satay

- Chiang Mai sausage with sticky rice (a local favorite)

- Khao soi noodle soup (a local favorite)

- Fermented ground pork fried with elephant garlic

- Stir fried twisted cluster beans with prawns

- Purple flower-shaped dumplings stuffed with chicken

- North-eastern style spicy clear soup with chicken

- Stir fried Thai herbs and chili with herbs

- Grilled marinated pork in hot dish with tamarind sauce

- Stir fried morning glory with oyster sauce and garlic

- Spicy papaya salad

- Steam pork ribs with salted soya beans dip

- Deep fried sun dried pork

The three chilis system

Levels of spiciness in Thai food are indicated by red chilis on the menu. There can be none, one, two or three chilis, depending upon the level of heat. You can request these in Thai if you wish (add krub or kaa to make it more polite):

- No chilis   *Kho mai sai phrik*

- One chili   *Kho sai phrik nit dieo*

- Two chilis   *Kho say prik song met*

- Three chilis kho say prik saam met

13: Two or Three Days in Chiang Mai

If like many visitors you have only two or three days in Chiang Mai on a limited budget, how can you best spend you time? Here is a short list of the 'must do and see' things in Chiang Mai, from elephants to walks.

Maesa Elephant Camp

The best-known elephant camp in the area, with three 'shows' daily where the elephants play soccer, build a log wall, burst balloons with darts and paint pictures, which can be purchased after the show. You can also book an elephant ride for two persons – about 30 minutes. You sit on a wooden seat on the back of the elephant. The elephants will steal and replace hats from tourists, and also accept tips – 20 baht is fine. They take the note from your hand with their trunk and carefully hand it to the mahout on their back.

The elephant camp is on the Mae Rim to Samoeng Rd, a few miles west of Mae Rim. About 40 minutes from town. 053 206-247. *Maesaelephantcamp.com.*

Patara Elephant Farm

This is an all-day visit in which your take care of 'your own elephant', so is very different to the Maesa Elephant Camp. You feed, clean, and ride your elephant, sitting on his or her neck like a mahout, not on an elephant seat. They will pick you up from your hotel. About 6,000 baht per person for the day ($200). Book early as it tends to fill up several weeks ahead – best to use the web site before you get to Chiang Mai.

299/22 Mae Hea, Chiang Mai. 081 992-2551 *Pataraelephantfarm.com*

Doi Suthep Temple

Wat Phra That Doi Suthep is the best known temple in Chiang Mai. If you plan to visit just one temple, make it this one. It's on a big hill a few miles outside of town.

There is a great chedi (a stupa or dome shaped structure) in the upper level, built in the 14th to 16th century. It is traditional to circle the chedi three times in a clockwise direction.

The views from the upper level extend over the whole of Chiang Mai.

Insider tip: You can take a tuk-tuk or taxi to the temple. To reach the temple there are over 300 stairs, but you can take a funicular to the top for a small fee. It is not well signposted but it is on the right of the main entrance.

City walks

There are two fairly short city walks that are of particular interest, with good restaurants, bars and shopping.

Tha Phae Road. Start on Chang Klan road, near the Dusit Princess, Le Meridien and the Starbucks store. Walk north (left from the Dusit Princess and Le Meridien, towards the Night Bazaar building) and note the shops and stalls on the way.

Turn left onto Tha Phae Road. Just on the left is Dan Collections Buddha shop, where all of the Buddhas are blessed in the temple before sale. A little further, past the pedestrian crossing, is the Raming Tea Shop on the right, and Wat Bupparam on the left (the big white wall). Note the Donald Duck figure in the temple garden!

There are some silver shops on the left, followed by the Thai Elephant Care Center, where you can book for the Maesa elephant camp. Then comes Nova, a contemporary silver jewelry store offering custom designs.

[114]

Cross the road to Book Zone, two traditional elephant bell shops (hand written signs outside), and Herb Basics.

A little further along is Elements, two inexpensive jewelry shops next to each other, with no name over the doors. On the corner is Boots the Chemist.

Turn right just past Boots to Chang Moi Kao, a small road with many second hand bookstores.

Thai Phae Gate is just in front of you, sometimes with market stalls. If you think it's time for a drink there is a Starbucks on the right just before the gate, or go through the gate to Moon Muang Rd, where you will find Coffee Club and Black Canyon Coffee.

Return to Tha Phae Road and turn left along the outside of the moat about two blocks to Loi Kroh Rd. On the way you will pass a Fish Spa, where customers put their bare feet in a tank and fish nibble the dead skin. Then Spotlight, a night time Go-Go bar.

Insider tip: If you go to a fish spa look for one that is clean, and with small black fish. The small fish are better at nibbling your feet than bigger fish.

Loi Kroh Road is also known as 'the bar street' with many bars and restaurants along its length, including The Rose Bar and Why Not. On the left is Chez Marco is a popular French bistro, followed by Rock Me Burgers, a modern burger restaurant. Further down on the right is the Chiang Mai Saloon (a cowboy bar with good burgers) and the Chiang Mai Entertainment Center, also known as the Boxing Complex, home of many bars including a ladyboy bar and a Go-Go bar. Continue until you reach Chang Klan Rd and Le Meridien and you have completed the circuit.

Insider tip: If you don't want to walk the length of Loi Kroh Road back to Le Meridien, it's easy to get a tuk tuk back for about 60 baht. ($2)

Charoenrat Road is the second suggested walk. It is in Watkate, just over the road from the Nawarat Bridge.

From the Night Bazaar street (Chang Klan Road), turn right and cross over the Nawarat Bridge. Turn left onto Charoenrat Road. This area is called Watkate. Wawee Coffee is on your left, and the Rarinjinda spa (good massages) on your right. Then on your left are Deck One, The Riverside and The Good View (three good restaurants). Craft Beer Factory is over the road from The Riverside (imported craft beers).

The Escudo Supper Club is next on the left – busy late at night. Then on the right are two lifestyle shops in old Portugese colonial buildings – Vila Cini and Oriental Style.

The budget-friendly B2 hotel is next on the left, followed by the Sala Lanna boutique hotel. A little further on the right is Woo, a flower-filled coffee shop with good drinks and snacks. The pink house opposite Woo is Vieng Joom On, a popular teahouse. Colour Factory is one of the last shops on the right, where you can paint model elephants.

At the end of the road, just before the tall Rimping Condominium, turn left across the Nakorn Ping Bridge, and then turn left again into Warorot Market. This is a busy market selling flowers, fruit, produce, clothing and electronics etc.

Continue straight, past the Police Station, the TOT telephone office and the Post Office, until you cross over Tha Phae Road and rejoin Chang Klan Road – the Night Bazaar street.

Insider tip: There are many tuk-tuks in the market if you've had enough walking. There is a new footbridge (under construction at the time of writing), which connects Charoenrat Rd directly with Warorot market. Look for the entrance to the footbridge on the left after the pink teahouse. This cuts off several hundred yards in both directions.

River Cruise

Mae Ping River Cruise. You can choose a long tail boat, a traditional teak rice barge or a large boat for groups. Sit down and relax over fresh fruit or herb juice. Stop off at Thai Farmer's House. 8.30am – 5.30pm. Boat departs every hour. 13 Charoenprathet Rd. 053 274-822. Email: Maepingrivercruise@hotmail.com. *Maepingrivercruise.com*

The Riverside

If you have only two or three nights in Chiang Mai, go to the Riverside on one of those nights. It's the most popular Thai / Western restaurant in town, on the banks of the Ping River. Mostly English speaking staff. Their less busy Craft Beer Factory (a second restaurant with imported draft beers) is just over the road, with a nice garden and waterfall. Both restaurants have soft jazz early and a rock band starting at 9.30pm. Easy walk from town via the Nawarat bridge. 9 Charoenrat Rd, Watkate. 053 243-239. *Theriversidechiangmai.com*

14: Staying Longer in Chiang Mai

Chiang Mai is great for a short visit, but what about staying longer? Perhaps a month or several months? The Thai 'no visa required' tourist entry gives you permission to stay in Thailand for up to 30 days (29 nights). To stay longer you need to apply to your local Thai embassy or consulate for a visa. 12 month visas are available, though they usually have a requirement to check in with the local Thai immigration office (or leave the country and re-enter) every 90 days.

Or if you have a 30 day stay you can make a 'visa run' to a neighboring border before your time is up, and re-enter Thailand for another 30 days.

There are several hotels offering discounts from their already reasonable rates for longer stays, the Dusit Princess and the B2, to name two. Another alternative is to rent an apartment or condo for a month or more. There are many apartment rental agencies, most of which speak English.

Westerners often move to Thailand to teach English and choose Chiang Mai because it is quieter and more beautiful than Bangkok. An average teaching salary in Chiang Mai at a government school is usually about 20,000 baht a month ($575). A one bedroom apartment in Chiang Mai will cost about 10,000 baht a month ($285).

Service Apartments

The Airport Greenery. Serviced apartment. Daily or monthly available. Swimming pool, restaurant and meeting room. Great location, one minute from the airport. Opposite Central Airport Plaza. 053 271-271. *Airportgreenery.com.*

The Grand Napat. Serviced apartment. 70/1 MuenDamPrakot Rd. 053 231-777.

TL Residence. Daily, weekly, monthly. 194 Mahidol Rd. 053 274-629. Email: reservation@thetlresidence.com.

Apartment Rental Agencies

Swed Home. Rent or sale. Brand new furnished condos. 207/2 Moobaan Nai Fun 3, Moo 3. 053 383-763. *Swedhomechiangmai.com*

Temporary office work spaces

You cannot work in Thailand without a work visa, but if you are just 'working from home' or working on your novel, for example, you will be fine. Here are some of the Chiang Mai temporary work spaces.

Starwork. A relaxing hidden space in the city. Fun atmosphere. Facilities include an outdoor workspace, pantry, and a waterfall! 87/9 Tunghotel Rd, Wat Ket. 053 307-000 *Starworkingchiangmai.com*

Bibie. Open 24/7. Free snacks and hot coffee. Hillside Condo 2, Nimmanhaemin Rd, Soi 9. 080 494-9944 *Facebook: Bibie Coworking & Sharing Space.*

MANA. A quiet and peaceful environment to work. Fresh coffee all day. 28/12 Nimmanhaemin Rd. 095 452-9014 *Facebook: MANA Co-working and Reading Space.*

Food Delivery

Food delivery services will pick up from many restaurants in town and deliver to you.

Foodpanda. *Foodpanda.co.th*

Meals on Wheels. 084 608-6661. *Mealsonwheels4u.com*

Chiang Mai Delivery. 081 026-6567. *Chiangmaidelivery.com.*

Thai Language Schools

A.U.A. Learn conversational Thai with native speakers. Established 1985. Group or individual instruction. 73 Rajadamnern Rd. 053 277-951 *Learnthaiinchiangmai.com*

Schools

Nakornpayap International School. (NIS). 240 Moo 6 San Phi Sua. 053 110-680. *Nis.ac.th*

Wichai Wittaya. Bilingual school. Nursery – grade 12. 264/1 Chang Klan Rd. 053 274-468. *Chai.ac.th*

Lanna International School. (LIST) University of Cambridge International Examinations. Email: Admissions@lannaist.ac.th. *Lannaist.ac.th*

Varee Chiang Mai School. Thai and modern dance clubs. World cup soccer. Cooking school. University of Cambridge International Examinations. 053 140-232. *Varee.ac.th*

15: Out of Town Trips

Mae Rim

Mae Rim is about 30 minutes out of town on highway 107, a reasonable taxi, car or motorbike ride. Turn left onto the Mae Rim – Samoeng Road (highway 1098) to the Four Seasons for lunch at Terraces restaurant, if that is in your budget, or a few miles further to the Maesa Elephant Camp, for elephant rides and shows. The Queen Sirikit Botanical Garden is further on the same road.

Lamphun

Lamphun is just 26 km out of Chiang Mai on highway 106. It is one of the nearest towns to Chiang Mai. Sites include Wat Phra That Haripunchai, an ancient monastery, and Ban Nong Chang Kuen, with extensive longan orchards. There is a longan festival in early May at the city's main stadium.

The Ban Wiang Yong Handicraft Village is right across the river from Lamphun town. On road 106 from Lamphun is the Pa Sang Handicraft Center, with handmade cotton items.

Lampang

After visiting Lamphun you can continue in the same direction to the larger city of Lampang. Lampang is well known for elephants and ceramics, and Buddhist temples in Burmese style. It is about 95 km from Chiang Mai on highway 11 – about an hour by car.

Lampang is Thailand's only city where horse-drawn carriages are in regular use as transport and can be seen waiting on street corners throughout the city. There are many traditional Thai houses in the Wiang Nua district.

Lampang's busy commercial area is on the south bank of the river. On weekends there is a walking street on Kad Thonka, with many shops and restaurants.

The Thai Elephant Conservation Center is 32 km from Lampang on highway 11 back towards Lamphun. The center cares for more than 50 elephants, and runs an elephant hospital.

Chiang Rai

Chiang Rai is on the Mae Kok river about 200 km (120 miles) northwest of Chiang Mai. There is no air service from Chiang Mai to Chiang Rai (save via Bangkok), and the journey takes 3.5 – 4 hours by car, motorbike or bus.

Chiang Rai is 66 km south of Mai Sai and the Myanmar (Burmese) border, and 55 km south of the Golden Triangle. The Golden Triangle is the border area of Myanmar (Burma), Laos and Thailand, and until recently was one of the world's leading areas of opium cultivation. The best time to visit Chiang Rai is in the cool season, November through February.

The population of Chiang Rai city is about 200,000, and there are about a million people in the province.

There is a Night Bazaar in the middle of downtown with about 40 restaurants. A place for souvenirs and local products. The Saturday night walking street is just north of downtown for crafts and food, with local dancers.   There is a large well-presented Opium

Museum, giving the history of opium production in the Golden Triangle area.

Lion Hill is the site of a Buddhist cave where hikers can walk right through a hill beside the Mae Kok river.

There is a Four Seasons Hotel in town, known as the 'Four Seasons Tented Camp'. It shares an elephant camp with the neighboring Anantara Hotel.

Mae Sai

Mae Sai is the northernmost city in Thailand, mainly a stepping stone for visits to Myanmar (Burma), with a river bridge at the border.

There is a bus service to and from Chiang Rai, which takes 90 minutes, and runs every 30 minutes. The town is quite small and can easily be covered on foot.

Most tourist Thailand on a 30 day (29 nights) visa-free entry. If you wish to extend your stay, the easiest method is to do a *visa run* to the nearest border, and for much of Thailand that is Mae Sai. It is only necessary to exit Thailand, re-enter Thailand and get your passport stamped. It can take just a few minutes. There are visa run buses that run to Mae Sai most days of the week from Chiang Mai.

The border crossing is to Tachileik province in Myanmar. An entry permit valid for up to 14 days costs $10 US.   Passports are held at the border until you return to Thailand (don't worry, you will get it back!) However if you are merely crossing the border to exit and re-enter Thailand (for a visa run), you can walk across the street, pick up your passport, and walk directly back across the bridge into Thailand.

Luang Prabang

Luang Prabang in Laos requires an airline flight, but it takes just 55 minutes to fly there from Chiang Mai on Lao Air. They fly an ATR 72 Turboprop, a modern propeller aircraft. When you arrive in Luang Prabang you need to provide a passport picture for visa purposes, and a visa fee – about $35, payable in US dollars.

Luang Prabang is like Chiang Mai 30 years ago – no shopping malls or tall buildings! The whole town is preserved as a UNESCO Heritage Site, and is bordered by the Mekong and Khan rivers. Laos is French influenced, and there are many sidewalk cafes in the town.

The central 'tourist' area of Luang Prabang is small, and is easy to walk. The local currency is the kip, and there are about 8,000 kip to the US dollar. A typical tuk tuk ride is 50,000 kip ($6). There is one main street with tourist shops and market stalls, anchored by the Post Office at one end and the Three Nagas Hotel at the other. (Both good landmarks for tuk tuks). There are many pleasant riverside walks, as there is a river on either side of the main street, within a couple of blocks. There is a small bamboo bridge over the Khan River, which can be crossed.

Insider tip: Agree on the fare for a tuk-tuk before you get in. Show the driver the amount you are offering. On some smaller tuk tuks they ask you to sit at the front end of the passenger area so that the weight is evenly distributed.

The former Royal Palace on the main shopping street is now the National Museum, which can be visited for a small fee.

There are several boat trips on the Mekong river. The Pak Ou caves are a 90 minute boat ride away, and contain thousands of old Buddhas. (Note that there are many high concrete steps to get into the caves). A sunset boat trip is another good option.

Luang Prabang is cooler than Chiang Mai, so if you are there in the winter months (the main tourist season, October through February), it is best to take a sweater or a light jacket.

Hotels

Les 3 Nagas – Ideally situated in town, at one end of the main shopping street. Spacious rooms on both

sides of the road. Good restaurant. Sakkarine Rd.
071 253-888. *3-Nagas.com*

La Residence Phou Vao – Colonial hotel with polished
wooden floors. A five minute tuk tuk ride from town,
and they provide free transportation. Lao / Thai /
western Poolside restaurant and good Doc Champa
Bar. Phou Vao Road. 071 212-194.
Residencephouvao.com

Restaurants

L'Elephant – the best-known restaurant in town, on a
side street beside the Mekong. Lao and Western.
Ban Vat Nong. 071 252-482. *Elephant-restau.com*

Apsara – Nice riverside terrace, on the Khan river.
Lao and western. Good wine list. Lunch and dinner.
Kongkitsarath Rd. 071 254-670.

Le Café Ban Vat Sene – Popular coffee shop opposite
the school, on the main street. 071 252-482.

For more information on out of town trips from
Chiang Mai, refer to the book 'Weekend Road Trips
Around Chiang Mai', published by The Nation
newspaper, and available from Chiang Mai
bookstores.

16: Some Thai Phrases

Thai is a tonal language – words change depending on how you say them, for example with a rising or falling tone. So written Thai words and phrases are just a starting point. You need to hear how Thais actually say those words to be better understood.

The most important Thai phrases to learn are those for 'Hello' and 'Thank you', with Thai numbers probably being the next easiest to learn.

To make a Thai phrase more polite, you end it with 'krub' (sometimes sounds like 'krap') if you are a man, and 'kaa' if you are a woman. Note that it is not whether you are speaking to a man or a woman that is important here, it is whether *you* are a man or a woman.

Hello and thank you

Hello, Sawasdee krub (male), Sawasdee kaa (female)

Thank you, kob koon (krub/kaa)

Numbers

Zero   Soon

One   Nung

Two	Song
Three	Sam
Four	Si
Five	Haa
Six	Hok
Seven	Jet
Eight	Bat
Nine	Kow
10	Sip
20	Yee sip (not song sip)
30, 40, 50 etc	Sam sip, Si sip, Haa sip, etc
100	Nung roi
200, 300 etc	Song roi, Si roi, etc
1000	Nung phan

Insider tip: The Thai word for 5 is haa, so when texting each other they often end the text with '555' – 'Ha ha ha!'

Days of the Week

Day	Wan
Monday	Wan Jaan
Tuesday	Wan Ang Karn
Wednesday	Wan Put
Thursday	Wan Paluehas
Friday	Wan Sook
Saturday	Wan Sao
Sunday	Wan Ar-tit

Dining

Table	Tao
Chair	Gao Eie
Plate	Jarn
Spoon	Shon
Fork	Sorm
Knife	Meed
Bowl	Charm
Glass	Gaew
Napkin	Pa Ched Pak

Plain water	Nam plao
Ice	Nam khoeng
Orange juice	Nam som khan

Colors

Color	See
Red	See Daeng
Yellow	See Leung
Pink	See Chom Poo
Green	See Kiew
Orange	See Som
Blue	See Fah
White	See Kao
Black	See Dum
Purple	See Muang

Useful Phrases

How are you?	Sabai dee reu?
Never mind	Mai pen rai

I cannot speak Thai	Phood Thai mai dai
Please speak slowly	Phood cha-cha
I don't understand	Mai kao jai
Where is the restroom?	Hong nam yoo tee nai?
Very expensive	Paeng maag
The bill please	Gep taang (krub/kaa)
Thank you very much	Kob khun maak
Today	Wan ni
Tomorrow	Prung ni
Yesterday	Mua wan ni

Places

Airport	Sanam bin
Railway station	Sa-tanee rot fai
Police station	Sa-tanee tum-ruad
Hotel	Rong-raem
Hospital	Rong-payabaan
Market	Talaad

Thai Insider: Chiang Mai

17: Useful Chiang Mai Information

Electricity

Thailand uses 220 volts, 50 cycles, and uses sockets that accept two pin flat or round plugs. Therefore phone chargers with US plugs will work, and those from the UK require an adapter. Appliances such as heated hair tongs and hair dryers designed for US voltage will not work, as the Thailand voltage is higher.

Phone numbers

Chiang Mai phone numbers (land lines) begin with the 053 area code, and then six digits, for example 053 555-123. This looks like 'one number is missing' to western eyes, but it is correct. (Recently, the 052 area code has been added). Mobile phone numbers have an area code like 069 or 086, and then seven digits, for example 069 555-1234. Bangkok numbers begin with 02.

The international dialing code is 001. Therefore for international calls you would dial the following:

USA   001 1

UK   001 44

Canada	001 1
Australia	001 61
New Zealand	001 64
Ireland	001 353

Sim Cards

To make local calls more cheaply, you can replace the SIM card in your phone with a Thai SIM card, and get a Thai number. However, if you do this, of course your 'home' mobile number will no longer be active. You can buy a prepaid SIM card from an AIS, True or DTAC store in a shopping center, and you can add money to your card at any 7-11 store in town.

Some Useful Chiang Mai Phone Numbers

Accident 1193

Ambulance 1669

Fire 199

Tourist police 1155 / 053 247-318

Lost car 1192

Directory Enquiries 183

Customs 053 270-660

Post Office 053 245-376

Chiang Mai Police 053 814-313

Provincial Police 053 140-000

City Hall 053 112-708

Chiang Mai Hospitals

There are many hospitals in Chiang Mai. Ram Hospital and Bangkok Hospital Chiang Mai are the best known for westerners.

Chang Puak Hospital 053 220-022

Chiang Mai Central Memorial 053 277-090

Chiang Mai Dental Hospital 053 411-150

Chiang Mai Ram Hospital 053 224-861

Bangkok Hospital Chiang Mai 052 089-817

St Peter Eye Hospital 053 225-011
Klai Mor Hospital 053 200-002

McCormick Hospital 053 241-311

Mother & Child Hospital 053 272-256

Theppanya Hospital 053 852-590

Embassies & Consulates

Most government offices in Thailand operate 8.30am to 4.30pm Monday to Friday. Foreign embassies and consulates may have different opening hours.

Bangkok embassies

US embassy. 95 Wireless Rd, Bangkok. 02 205-4000

UK embassy. 14 Wireless Rd, Bangkok. 02 305-8333

Canadian embassy. 15/F Abdulrahim Place, Bangkok. 02 636-0560

Australian embassy. 37 Th Sathorn Tai, Bangkok. 02 344-6300

New Zealand embassy. 87 Wireless Rd, Bangkok. 02 254-2530

Singapore embassy. 129 Th Sathorn Tai, Bangkok. 02 286-2111

Chiang Mai Consulates

Consulate General of the USA, 387 Wichanond Rd, Chiang Mai Regular number: 053 107-777. Emergency number (death, arrest, etc) 053 107-777. After-hours emergency (081 881-1878). Online appointments are necessary for most things (passports, notary, etc). *Email acschn@state.gov. Chiangmai.usconsulate.gov*

Consulate of Great Britain. 198 Bumrungraj Rd. 053 263-015.

Consulate of Australia. 236 Chiang Mai – Doi Saket Rd. Sansai. 053 492-480.

Consulate of Canada. 151 Moo 4, Super Highway, Thasala. 053 850-147

Airports

The code for the main Bangkok airport (Suvarnabhumi) is BKK, and for Chiang Mai it is CNX. Note that the 'old' Bangkok airport, Don Muang (also known as Don Mueang), is still operating, and the code for that is DMK. Don Muang is the regional hub for Nok Air, Thai Air Asia, Thai Lion Air and Orient Thai Airways. Suvarnabhumi (the main international airport) is the regional hub for Thai airways and almost all of the other airlines operating in Thailand.

Insider tip: Flights to Chiang Mai depart from both Suvarnabhumi and Don Muang airports, so do not assume that you are leaving from the main airport. Check your flight number. If it is has three digits you are departing from Suvarnabhumi, if it has four digits you are departing from Don Muang.

Chiang Mai has direct international flights, so it is not always necessary to arrive or depart Thailand via

Bangkok. Chiang Mai's direct flights include Hong Kong, Macau, Singapore, Seoul and Luang Prabang in Laos.

If you arrive in Thailand via Bangkok and proceed directly to Chiang Mai you will pass through immigration in Bangkok but clear customs in Chiang Mai. You will be given a 'CIQ' sticker in Bangkok, and upon arrival in Chiang Mai you will be directed to International Arrivals, and not Domestic Arrivals. There you will pick up your luggage and clear customs.

Arriving by Rail

There is a good rail service from Bangkok to Chiang Mai. There are overnight trains leaving Bangkok's Hua Lamphong Station at 4.30pm and arriving at Chiang Mai station, to the east of the city, the next morning. *Railway.co.th*

Insider tip: The Eastern Orient Express train travels regularly from Singapore, through Malaysia, to Bangkok. A couple of times a year, the train makes the additional journey in luxury from Bangkok to Chiang Mai.

Arriving by Bus

There is an air-conditioned bus service from Bangkok to Chiang Mai. It departs from the Mo Chit bus station, next to the Mo Chit station of the elevated Bangkok sky train.

Changing Money

You can change money from your local currency to Thai baht at your hotel, or at one of the many 'Exchange' windows in town. They will not accept torn, crumpled or defaced notes, so bring clean new notes if you can. Thai baht notes come in values of 20, 50, 100, 500 and 1,000 baht

Credit cards

Credit cards are widely accepted at larger stores and hotels in Thailand, particularly Visa and Mastercard, and to a lesser extent, American Express. Cash only is accepted in small stores and all markets. Small bills are useful. Credit cards can be used in most ATMs to withdraw Thai currency (which will usually be in 1,000 baht notes). Should you lose your card, call one of these numbers:

Visa: 001 800-441-3485

Mastercard: 001 800-11-887-0663.

American Express: 02 273-5222

Diner's Club: 02 238-3660

Thai Insider: Chiang Mai

18: Authors' Bios

Granville Kirkup is a former business and popular restaurant owner. He has been visiting Chiang Mai for almost thirty years, and has seen it change much over the years. Ten years ago he purchased a condominium in Chiang Mai, on the Ping River, and he now lives there for part of every year. Married with two children, he lives with his wife, Sidney, in California when they are not in Chiang Mai.

Email: *Granvillekirkup2017@gmail.com*

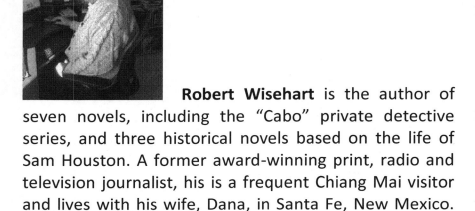

Robert Wisehart is the author of seven novels, including the "Cabo" private detective series, and three historical novels based on the life of Sam Houston. A former award-winning print, radio and television journalist, his is a frequent Chiang Mai visitor and lives with his wife, Dana, in Santa Fe, New Mexico. *Robertwisehart.com*

19: Acknowledgments

Many locals, expats and frequent Chiang Mai visitors have helped to provide the information and Insider Tips in this book. Among these are Julie Hastings, Armelle Chungchareonsuk-Pennors, Sidney Kirkup, Dana Wisehart, Louise Kirkup, John Rees, Arthur Wickson, Tricia Freeman, Pamela Terrones, David Rueda, Aimee Richter, Katie Rollins, Jeff Rollins, Susan Davis, David Schmidt, Gerald Maguire MD, Connie Yeaman, Alam Horner, Jessica Scott, Veronica Nanko, Bill Horner, Barbara Haywood, Pakin Ployphicha, Toby Allen, Patcharin Toon, Richard Kirkup, Monica Hampton, Sophie & Larry Cripe, Don & Mary Yeaman, Richard Dixon, Manat Chowmuang, Harriett Stanley, Cheryl Hoenemeyer, Annie Frome, Howard & Annie Freedland.

The maps are used by kind permission of Chang Puak Magazine, Chiang Mai. *Changpuakmagazine.com.*

Comments, updates and corrections are much appreciated, and will be acknowledged here in a future edition. Please send an email to the authors at *GranvilleKirkup2017@gmail.com.*

20: Further Reading

Retiring in Thailand. Live in paradise for pennies on the dollar. Sunisa Wongdee Terlecky & Philip Bryce. Paiboon Bangkok Publishing. paiboonpublishing@gmail.com *Paiboonpublishing.com*

Burma's Golden Triangle. Andre & Louis Boucard. Asia Books. 5 Sukhumvit Soi 61, Bangkok. PO Box 40. Bangkok 10110.

Thailand Customs & Culture. Roger Jones. (One of a series on customs and culture in different countries). Kuperand. *Culturesmart.co.uk*

Successful Living in Thailand. Roger Welty. Asia Books. Information@asiabooks.com *Asiabooks.com*

A Year in Chiang Mai. Alexander Gunn. The Life Change People Co Ltd. *Booksmango.com*

Exploring Chiang Mai (4th edition). Oliver Hargreaves. Within Books. Within Design Co, Chiang Mai. within@within.co.th *Within.co.th*

Insight Pocket Guide, Chiang Mai. Published 1992, updated 2003. *Insightguides.com*

What's What in a Wat. Carol Stratton. Silkworm Books. Chiang Mai. info@silkwormbooks.com. *Silkwormbooks.com*

Weekend Road Trips around Chiang Mai. The Nation. Monote@Nationgroup.com. *Nationmultimedia.com*

Enchanting Chiang Mai & Northern Thailand. Mick Shippen. John Beaufoy Publishing. *Johnbeaufoy.com*

Nancy Chandler's Map of Chiang Mai. The definitive local map. *Nancychandler.net*

Ancient Luang Prabang. Denise Haywood. River Books. Bangkok. riverps@ksc.th.com *Riverbooksbk.com*

Made in the USA
Columbia, SC
31 March 2018